GLOBAL ORGANIZED CRIME:

The New Empire of Evil

GLOBAL ORGANIZED CRIME:

The New Empire of Evil

EDITORS: LINNEA P. RAINE
& FRANK J. CILLUFFO

CSIS CENTER FOR STRATEGIC AND INTERNATIONAL STUDIES

The Center for Strategic and International Studies (CSIS), founded in 1962, is an independent, tax-exempt, public policy research institution based in Washington, D.C.

The mission of the Center is to advance the understanding of emerging world issues in the areas of international economics, politics, security, and business. It does so by providing a strategic perspective to decision makers that is integrative in nature, international in scope, anticipatory in its timing, and bipartisan in its approach. The Center's commitment is to serve the common interests and values of the United States and other countries around the world that support representative government and the rule of law.

Library of Congress Cataloging-in-Publications Data
Global organized crime : the new empire of evil / editors, Frank J.
    Cillufo & Linnea P. Raine.
        p.   cm.
  ISBN 0-89206-312-2
    1. Organized crime—Congresses.   2. Organized crime—Prevention—
Congresses.   I. Cillufo, Frank J.   II. Raine, Linnea P.
III. Center for Strategic and International Studies (Washington,
D.C.)
HV6441.G57   1994
364.1'06—dc20   94-41954
                                                                 CIP

ISBN 0-89206-312-2

The Center for Strategic and International Studies
1800 K Street, N.W., Washington, D.C. 20006
Telephone: (202) 887-0200
Fax: (202) 775-3199

Contents

Ronald Murphy
Director, Advanced Systems
Advanced Research Projects Agency, DoD

Robert H. Kupperman
Project Codirector, CSIS

R. James Woolsey
Director of Central Intelligence

Cert Coordination Center
L. Dain Gary

The Wild West of NETSEC–Between Warning and Disaster
Donn B. Parker

Countering the Computer Intrusion Threat
Jim Christy

Fissile Material Proliferation
David Kay

Executive Summary

The dimensions of global organized crime present a greater international security challenge than anything Western democracies had to cope with during the cold war. Worldwide alliances are being forged in every criminal field from money laundering and currency counterfeiting to trafficking in drugs and nuclear materials. Global organized crime is the world's fastest growing business, with profits estimated at $1 trillion.

These were some of the conclusions of CSIS's conference on Global Organized Crime held in Washington, D.C. on September 26, 1994. The event brought together leaders of the financial, intelligence, and law enforcement communities.

Keynote speaker Louis Freeh, the director of the FBI, stressed that "the ravages of transnational crime" are the greatest long-term threat to the security of the United States" and warned that the very fabric of democratic society was at risk everywhere.

The director of Central Intelligence, R. James Woolsey, reinforced all the speakers and panelists with these words: "The threats from organized crime transcend traditional law enforcement concerns. They affect critical national security interests ... some governments find their authority besieged at home and their foreign policy interests imperiled abroad."

Law enforcement and national security have become increasingly indistinguishable. But the laws have not kept up with the new breed of transnational criminals and their high-tech methodologies.

To develop short- and long-term strategies and mechanisms that will come to grips with these emerging national security concerns, CSIS has launched a major program on Global Organized Crime. Various task forces will examine the critical parameters of each transnational crime problem and identify specific recommendations for policy, legislation, technology, and organization.

Some of the points made at the conference:

- Operational and intelligence gathering techniques employed by transnational criminals are more sophisticated than those of law enforcement agencies.
- Some 5,700 Russian criminal gangs dominate every aspect of political, economic, and social life in the former Soviet republics. More than 200 of them have established relations with counterparts in 29 other countries, including the United States.
- Intelligence assets recently exposed an academy in Bulgaria that teaches about and perfects computer viruses.
- The illegal export of raw materials alone reportedly costs the Russian

government $10 billion in lost revenues per year.

- Money laundering is now estimated at $500 billion a year.
- There is one woman with a high school diploma who is the regulator for 520 commercial banks in the Cayman Islands.
- Counterfeiting of U.S. tender increased 300 percent between 1992 and 1993.
- Counterfeit currency is being used to fund terrorist activities throughout the world. For example, between Iraq and Iran alone, they have counterfeited $10 billion worth of near perfect $100 bills.
- The Financial Crimes Division of the Secret Service estimates that Nigerian criminal groups account for more than $2.5 million in credit card fraud a month in Dallas alone.
- Financial crimes are now threatening the world's financial infrastructure.
- Tomorrow's villain or despot armed with a computer and a small squad of expert hackers can be as dangerous and as disruptive as any adversary we have faced since World War II.
- Criminal computer intrusions have grown from 132 in 1990 to an average of 195 per month in 1994. Less than five percent of compromised computer systems even realize they have been penetrated.
- Computer software technology is changing every 12 to 18 months; hardware, every 36 to 48 months. International criminals buy state of the art; law enforcement agencies lag five years behind.
- "Information anarchy" on the superhighway is enabling criminal employees to take control of a corporation's assets from management through superior encryption skills.
- One "hacker" mounted 26 days of "attacks" on U.S. Air Force computers from 10 different points of origin and at least eight countries, transferred data from the South Korean Atomic Research Institute, and penetrated NASA, the jet propulsion laboratory in California, and the Goddard Space Flight Center in Maryland—before he was caught in a third-floor walkup in London. He was 16 years old.
- Some 65,000 computers in Europe were compromised in one weekend—by one person "hacking" out of Australia.
- Iraq's Saddam Hussein, using computers and super hackers, could paralyze a number of vital nerve centers in the United States.
- There have been some 400 attempts to sell nuclear materials in Germany in the past two years.
- There is a large pool of nations and criminal organizations that are now in the market for nuclear materials.

Opening Remarks

Arnaud de Borchgrave
Project Director, CSIS

Ladies and gentlemen, good morning. I am the Center for Strategic and International Studies' project director on Global Organized Crime, arguably the world's fastest growing industry—and they spend very little on office supplies.

We have seen many fascinating phenomena since the end of the cold war, some encouraging, some disquieting, but only one truly alarming. After the great Soviet meltdown and the erosion of the nation state and the breakdown of the discipline generated by a fear that we no longer fear, we have witnessed an astonishing proliferation of international crime syndicates and the global alliances that they have created.

As legitimate businesses understood and adjusted to the complexities of this new global marketplace, so did international criminal organizations, the illegitimate businesses they control, and, increasingly, the legitimate businesses they penetrate.

Transnational crime chiefs are busy carving up our little planet into privileged sanctuaries for everything from counterfeiting and credit card forgeries to money laundering and the smuggling of radioactive materials as well as illegal immigrants. They have become so brazen that they are a little bit like the guy in a department store trying on nylons over his head.

This summer's weapons grade plutonium contraband scare in Germany was just the tip of the iceberg, but law enforcement capabilities still stop at meaningless frontiers ignored by transnational crime, which moves like information and money in this age of ever faster and ever more powerful computers, at the speed of light.

The head of the German FBI, the BKA, was in Washington on May 25th, and he told a congressional committee that we are literally in a race against time. What we have undertaken at CSIS, beginning today, I think is unique in its global scope. We do not wish to compete with or duplicate what others are doing. Nor is it our job to criticize, knowing that criticism is simply prejudice made plausible. But we do plan to analyze and become a catalyst that will enable democratic societies to take the actions required to cope with what Senator Nunn has described as potentially a far more serious threat than any faced during the cold war—next to which Haiti, of course, is not even a blip on our radar screen.

And now to introduce someone who does not need any introduction, David Abshire, president of CSIS and the man who founded this results-oriented institution in 1962 at the height of the Cuban missile crisis. Dr. Abshire, as you know, has been in and out of government, always in positions of high responsibility, where he broke the mold of politics and diplomacy being the art of the possible because the word impossible does not belong in his vocabulary.

Welcome

David M. Abshire
President, CSIS

I do not want this to become mutual admiration, but I do want to voice a real note of appreciation to Arnaud. You know, as we use this word strategic, it means different things to different people. And one of the things it means to us is staying ahead of the issues and then bringing together the diverse factors that come to bear on a given issue. Arnaud de Borchgrave has been going around CSIS for three years now—we have 160 people that cover the entire world on many domestic issues—and he has constantly harped on this global crime issue and its importance. The culmination of these warnings is this meeting and the work that has gone into it, and there will be much more in terms of a program that will come out of it. So, he has been ahead of his time in warning and analyzing and talking and integrating this most important issue into our work, whether it is on security or finance or trade or other issues.

Next, I want to thank young Frank Cilluffo, Jr., who has done the detailed conference work with Janet Davis. And, finally, I want to thank Bill Webster, a distinguished member of our Advisory Board at CSIS, which is chaired by Paul Volcker. You know Bill by his extraordinary record as a federal judge, as director of the FBI, and as director of Central Intelligence in an extremely difficult time in the wake of the Iran contra affair. His leadership, his honesty, his integrity, and his judgment, they shine through in this city of Washington. And with that judgment and leadership, Arnaud and I could think of no better person to chair this effort, to chair our steering group, and to help us to get the issues right and get at them in the most appropriate fashion.

Chairman's Introduction

William Webster
Milbank, Tweed, Hadley & McCloy
Former Director of Central Intelligence and the
Federal Bureau of Investigation

This is, in a sense, a beginning and a very, very important beginning. It is not a one-day issue that we are going to go away and forget about. We hope to have come together with a better consensus on the nature of the threat and the means of dealing with it before this day is over, and we have an outstanding group of people to make presentations. You have the programs and you have the bios, so I will not presume on your time to talk about them.

It is clear that, unless we have a better understanding—call it intelligence, call it understanding—of what is out there, this country and other countries in the free world are going to experience major setbacks. If we do have a better understanding and a strategy for dealing with it, we hope to achieve some of the successes internationally that we were able to achieve in this country, knowing that we still have much to do.

Back in 1960, 34 years ago, as a new United States attorney for eastern Missouri under President Eisenhower, I asked the special agent in charge of the FBI office in St. Louis to come to see me and brief me on organized crime. His response was very simple and succinct. There is no such thing as organized crime, only some loose familial relationships. That was two years after Appalachia, and that was, in many respects, the sum level of our understanding.

Thanks in part to the wisdom of Clarence Kelly in identifying organized crime as one of the areas in which the FBI should spend its time effectively, and to the nine years that I was there, we opened up fissures in all of the organized crime families. We knew that we had not completed the job, which was continued with vigor by Bill Sessions and now by Judge Freeh.

During that time, we were looking for people of real distinction among the younger special agents, the future stars of the Bureau, and it quickly came to my attention that a young special agent had performed in an outstanding way in investigating labor racketeering on the east coast. (We called it UNIRAC.) I had the pleasure of giving Louis Freeh an important award at that time. It was not too long after that the southern district of New York discovered what an outstanding special agent we had and persuaded Louis to come and work as an assistant U.S. attorney.

Louis is a graduate of Rutgers, both college and law school, was Phi Beta Kappa, and later obtained a master's degree in criminal law at New York University. He is eminently qualified, both in terms of experience and ability, and he found himself in charge of the investigation of what became known as "the Pizza Connection." This was our first indication, and an important first indication, that major Sicilian organized crime groups were working, and working effectively, within the United States—not as part of La Cosa Nostra but as direct imports from Italy. This was the beginning of our real awareness of the international character of organized crime.

This spring, Judge Freeh gave very chilling testimony to the Congress on the nature of the threat, particularly with respect to organized crime groups coming out of what was the Soviet Union and the Soviet bloc. I will not presume to repeat that testimony because I hope that Judge Freeh will share some of that with us today.

Following that, Judge Freeh led a delegation to the former Soviet Union and its bloc countries—some nine in all, I believeson relationships with those countries. The FBI had always had a small number of liaison offices throughout the world, but, of course, never behind what was the Iron Curtain. He seized that moment to realize that this was one of the things that could be done on an international basis to cope with a growing problem that was not only threatening to destabilize the government in Russia but to do real damage in Germany and, indeed, in the United States and other countries throughout the world.

It is very timely, I think, that the present director of the FBI should come to us with this kind of experience, and we hope very much that, with his leadership and his input, those of us in this room can do serious work in dealing with one of the major threats to our national security in the future. It is a great privilege for me to introduce our good friend and my good friend, Judge Louis Freeh, director of the FBI.

International Organized Crime and Terrorism: From Drug Trafficking to Nuclear Threats

Louis J. Freeh
Director, Federal Bureau of Investigation

It is a pleasure to be here with you this morning and give you a couple of reflections and thoughts that I have on the very important subject matter that is before you today and hopefully in the days to come.

I know that many of you in the room have a wide variety of experience in this particular area and are very, very distinguished in the issues that are immediately before us with respect to a new problem that makes transnational crime an issue that it has never been before in the United States. Ten years ago when I was a prosecutor, a transnational crime was perhaps several hundred kilograms of narcotics or contraband moving across borders. The whole nature and scope and dimensions of transnational crime have changed so rapidly that we really have a new menu before us in terms of what is required and how we must react.

My remarks today are framed a little bit by the trip that Bill referred to. The trip was undertaken by myself, my good friend, DEA Administrator Tom Constantine, Treasury Under Secretary Ron Noble, Ambassador Bob Gelbard, and some other individuals. Over ten days, we visited nine nations. During the course of the trip, we met with the presidents of five separate countries as well as numerous ministers of the interior, police officials, prosecutors, and judges.

The trip took us first to Germany. From there, we went to Slovakia, the Czech Republic, Hungary, and Poland. From Poland, we went to Lithuania, where we met with representatives, not only of the Lithuanian government but of Estonia and Latvia, who sent their delegates. From there, we went to the Ukraine and, finally, to Russia, the trip concluding briefly in Austria.

At the outset of the trip, Assistant Secretary of State Dick Holbrooke, who was then United States ambassador to Germany, said that the trip symbolized the transition from cold war politics to the far more difficult issues of the post-cold war period.

People ask where is the post-cold war foreign policy. "The CIA and Defense Department issues that predominated during the cold war have receded," he said.

With respect to the countries we were about to visit, Assistant Secretary Holbrooke said, "Law enforcement is at the forefront of our national interest in this part of the world." He described it as "the evolving American foreign policy."

The purpose of the delegation's trip was quite simple: to ascertain and discuss common law enforcement issues and consider types of law enforcement assistance that the United States could provide to these newly emerging democracies. We all agreed that the results of the trips and the meetings exceeded all of our expectations. My colleagues and I were struck, of course, by the extent to which our law enforcement interests mirrored those of our foreign partners.

Each of the countries faces similar problems, including active organized crime and gangs, increased drug abuse and drug trafficking, widespread and innovative forms of money laundering activity, rising numbers of violent crimes, rising heroin addiction, counterfeiting, terrorist activities, and the ominous threat created by the illicit sale and diversion of nuclear materials.

Shortly after our delegation's trip, President Clinton met with foreign leaders, including President Yeltsin, during a trip to Europe that included the G-7 conference in Naples. The president noted that in his meetings security issues had a high priority and that there was general agreement on the need to coordinate efforts, especially in the fight against organized crime, drug trafficking, and money laundering. The president said, "These things now know no national boundaries. We think this is one area where we can work together and really do something that will benefit the citizens of our nations in Europe and the United States."

We know from our experience that criminal groups and terrorists strive to achieve two primary goals, power and money. Their unending chase for these goals threatens the emerging democracies and stability of central and eastern Europe, as well as the countries of the former Soviet Union. For example, law enforcement agencies have detected cooperation in the extremely lucrative drug trade between Russian organized crime groups and other criminal groups.

In 1993, Russian authorities intercepted a ton of South American cocaine that was being shipped to St. Petersburg. It was shipped there by Russian-Eurasian organized crime figures working very significantly in conjunction with Colombian drug cartels. The same year, in a DEA case, 15 Russian and Sicilian organized crime figures were convicted in this country in connection with a drug conspiracy that involved heroin being shipped to New York City, again from Warsaw, in conjunction with partners from both of those countries.

Nuclear materials provide another means by which criminals can readily achieve both power and money. Terrorist groups and outlaw nations provide a ready-made market prepared to pay top dollar for these commodities. The potential results of their obtaining such materials can only be described as catastrophic. The possibilities of the sale and diversion of nuclear materials are unfortunately now all too real.

During our meeting with President Walesa of Poland, he expressed great concern about nuclear blackmail. His concern, he told us, was not the possibility of terrorists getting hold of nuclear materials, but a criminal group getting materials and threatening to poison the water supply in an extortion attempt against the government of Poland—an attempt that he feared was not only possible but one that we were ill-prepared to face.

We know that such international law problems are not solved merely by intelligence community responses. It is not a matter any more of spy and counterspy. Instead, it requires a law enforcement response, including the establishment of police-to-police bridges and viable working relationships among and between police officers.

The nuclear seizures in Germany make my point. Those seizures were done by police officers using fundamental police law enforcement techniques such as undercover agents and informants—in one case in Germany the use of a Secret Service informant. Given the scope and magnitude of these problems, communication and cooperation among law enforcement investigators on an international basis is critical. The intelligence community has an important role to play. Nevertheless, the role, in my view, is one of support to and for our law enforcement community. Indeed, significant progress can be made only by turning such information into action.

We must remember that law enforcement officials in central and eastern Europe and the countries of the former Soviet Union are grappling with historical problems that will directly affect their ability to fight the criminals and crime groups currently operating in their midst. It will also affect our ability to work with those law enforcement officials. We are familiar with the Communist regimes that ruled those nations with an oppressive hand for many, many years. In light of their newly won liberty, we can easily understand the people's desire to cast off that yoke forever.

In these countries, there is a lingering perception of law enforcement as the enemy. For their part, the law enforcement officials that we met expressed a commitment to conduct their business professionally and in accordance with the rule of law. Some of those officials pointed out that they themselves had been oppressed by the prior regimes. These officials readily acknowledge their bad public image and their corruption problems. They also recognize the great potential that corruption can have on the effective carrying out of their mission. Their officers are poorly paid, and the spoils of crime can be very tempting there, as elsewhere. We learned, for instance, that in Estonia, police officers are paid the equivalent of about $70 per month.

I am mindful, however, of the words of Hungary's president, Arpad Goncz. He said that police corruption has not reached epidemic proportions all over eastern Europe despite some instances of it and some prevalence of it in particular places. He added that good law enforcement officers in those countries will seek out American law enforcement, and American law enforcement must seek to work with them.

President Goncz explained that those countries should not be avoided or abandoned merely on account of their problems with respect to official corruption. He is right, in my view. It is our responsibility to seek out people of integrity who are committed to domestic law enforcement. The alternative, walking away and ignoring the mounting crime problems, is no alternative at all.

There remains, however, a tension within these countries. On the one hand, there is an admitted need to stem the sweeping tide of crime. On the other hand, there is concern about providing the police with too much power. The scale with which these nations resolve this tension will directly affect their ability to function and survive as democracies. It will also have a direct impact on our willingness to forge law enforcement alliances with them. We found that these countries want to learn from the American experience. As Poland's President Lech Walesa said, they want to work and they want to understand how we do it in the United States. How does the FBI, for example, strike a balance between strong law enforcement and the protection of human rights?

Others expressed concerns about wire taps, concerns that are well founded in light of their histories. Nevertheless, those same persons recognize the value of wire taps as a legitimate law enforcement tool. Again, the question was asked, "How do you do it in America?"

President Vaclav Havel of the Czech Republic told us that, in the aftermath of communism, the Czech government had gone to great lengths to ensure that the police did not violate anyone's rights. He acknowledged, however, in light of increasing crime rates, that those sentiments had to be balanced with the need to allow the police to fight criminals effectively. These countries have extended a hand to us, a hand that, it seems to me, we need to grasp. If America's law enforcement agencies fail in that endeavor, we will have only ourselves to blame.

I am not talking about empowering the machinery of state oppression. I am talking about teaching legitimate law enforcement officers how to investigate in accordance with our fundamental democratic principles. Officials from each of the emerging democracies that we met felt that the range of American aid would be valuable in addressing their crime problems, including, specifically, training. Although the request for help included technical assistance, forensic training, investigative liaison, and cooperation, all the countries also requested the assignment of our federal law enforcement experts to their countries to assist in the development of cooperative anti-crime programs.

They made it clear, however, that the burden is not America's alone. Indeed, they made it clear that they want to be full partners in this effort. For their part, Germany and Austria and many other countries have generously offered their own help in conjunction with us to provide such assistance.

Throughout my careers as an FBI agent and a federal prosecutor, I have maintained a firm belief in cooperative law enforcement. Given the common and increasing crime problems facing the United States, central and eastern Europe, and the countries of the former Soviet Union, my belief has been strengthened with respect to the problems now before us in this part of the world. We must increase the training programs for our foreign police counterparts. These programs must be large enough to produce speedy results. It is in our best interest to have our personnel on the ground in those countries, training police forces that we can count on and training them according to the due process and democratic principles that serve us well here.

Congress has acknowledged the significance of those issues. Through the foresight of congressional leaders such as Senators Leahy, Domenici, and McConnell and Congressman Gilman, funding has been obtained so that the United States can develop a meaningful law enforcement plan of action. For this effort to succeed, further funding will be required. I know that there is a continued need to maintain our national security. Nonetheless, as I have said before, with the end of the cold war, it may be possible for all of the former cold war adversaries to now divert some of their cold war intelligence budgets toward priority law enforcement and crime reduction projects. That money would be well spent by the foreign governments, protecting people and ensuring that democratic institutions thrive. Given our shared problems, it would be money well spent here–protecting our own domestic security and our people from the ravages of transnational crime.

All of the former cold war adversaries should also consider reprogramming personnel and technologies to the fight against criminals and terrorists. Without new and enhanced levels of international law enforcement cooperation, each country will pay a terrible price if it tries to fight crime largely by itself. We can no longer revel in the euphoria associated with the dismantling of the Berlin Wall and the fall of the Iron Curtain. The United States government, especially its law enforcement components, must act now, swiftly and comprehensively, to aid these emerging democracies in central and eastern Europe, as well as those that formerly composed the Soviet Union. If we fail to seize that moment, the opportunities for liberty may well be lost. We cannot sit on the sidelines and witness a different form of gangster ascend to the pinnacles of power in those nations.

There is an old song that we all knew growing up, certainly in my generation, and that was that you did not have to be a weatherman to know that the weather had changed. With respect to international crime, with respect to the dimensions and characters now assaulting not just our own institutions but those abroad, it is clear to me that a fundamental sea change has taken place with respect to organized crime, and that is the severity, the complexity, the vast resources and organization that these groups now have. It is no longer simply a question of maintaining our traditional law enforcement models and paradigms and then trying to project those overseas.

In my view, what is required is a fundamental change in how we operate overseas as law enforcement entities. If we are spending billions of dollars overseas for intelligence purposes that are valid, we should be spending millions of dollars now for law enforcement purposes, because our own domestic security and our national security are gravely threatened by these types of crime, particularly nuclear counterproliferation.

My view is that the very, very traditional and very successful law enforcement techniques, such as the ones used by the BKA in the four seizures in Germany since May (with undercover agents, informants, sting operations) that result in arrests and prosecutions, and the development of informants—these are really the tools that should be at our forefront now.

Question and Answer Session

Mr. de Borchgrave: Thank you, Mr. Director. Could I ask you about your trip to Moscow, more specifically, how local law enforcement is allocated one liter of gasoline, apparently, per old Lada car to follow the bad guys driving around in the latest fast Western cars. How are they going to overcome this problem? In the discussions that you had with them, perhaps you could enlighten us.

Director Freeh: Well, they are quite aware not only of the fundamental defects in terms of equipment and resources but also painfully aware—from the minister of the interior on down—about the severe corruption problems that extend into many of the ranks of the police, both on the ground and managerially. I think what has to happen is a whole series of things. First of all, they need some fundamental laws with which to operate.

There are two packages in the Duma now. One is an anti-organized crime package. The other one is an anti-corruption package. If enacted, they would not only bring the Federation up to our standards but, in some cases, particularly in the area of corruption, would far surpass our own legal requirements.

What they do need, however, is the incentive to attract the best young men and women into that profession. The Moscow police are paid the equivalent of about $200 per month. Since 1991, 600 police officers have been killed in the line of duty, that is a number that is just overwhelming compared to our own statistics. What they have to do is what they have done in some of the police forces in Europe and successfully now in one component of the Hungarian police, raise the financial incentives for people who walk into that kind of an occupation. This is one way to attract people. They need to recruit. They need to train. They may need many years to get to where they need to be with respect to that. But the package in the Duma not only provides for increases in salary but resources that, heretofore, the ministry police, as opposed to the intelligence and security police, have not had in that country.

Dr. Abshire: When I was NATO in 1984, 1985, and 1986, we were hit, as you recall, by a wave of terrorists, and Bill Webster, who was director of the FBI, came over and there were a lot of international meetings. It was very difficult, politically, to get some of these governments to open up. You had some people in high places that were contributing through benign neglect and so forth in certain countries, and it was very difficult to build that cooperation. But, after about nine months, it did happen.

It seems to me that what you are dealing with is even more difficult, because in a variety of countries we have politicians at very high levels with some Mafia involvement. Is this going to take a much greater push at, say, the G-7 and heads of governments level to build the kind of momentum we need? That ultimately is what happened on terrorism within the Alliance countries during that period. I just wonder if—added to the trip that you and Secretary Holbrooke made—this thing is not going to have to be done at really at a very high level and involve parliaments as well.

Director Freeh: I think that is right. I think it is going to have to be continued in terms of momentum from the G-7 level. It certainly is going to be a topic at the summit this week between the two presidents. It should be the priority really of all those parliaments involved. It cannot be done on a lower level, although there are things that we can do on the working level to increase the motivation and the field of operation.

Just to give you an example, we were talking before I left Russia with the minister of the interior, and he said to me, very interestingly, you know, you now have several cases in the United States against Russian organized crime operations. I am sure from time to time you need Russian-speaking police officers to work against them. Why don't you think about taking one of my officers? I'll assign him to you. You work him undercover in the United States according to your own guidelines, and we will bring down the case together. If there are people in the United States to be arrested, you arrest them. If there are people to be arrested in Russia, we will arrest them.

It is those kinds of cases that will begin the momentum that has taken us from 1982, for instance, in Italy, where we did not work any cases together because the police forces did not trust each other in many cases, to a point where we routinely take down cases on both sides of the ocean at the same time, using each other's undercover agents and evidence. We are a long way from doing that in some of these eastern European countries, but I think if the pressure is maintained at the top and the resources are given, the police will do the job. The police will find on both sides of the equation partners with whom they can work effectively and reliably. And once we begin taking down cases like that, we will build the kind of relationship that will catch fire—as it did in Italy—and achieve really unprecedented results. But the pressure on the top has to maintain itself for the necessary resources. We cannot do this on a shoestring budget, and we are not talking about a lot of money. We are not talking about billions of dollars. We are talking about money necessary to make this relationship real.

Mr. de Borchgrave: Mr. Federmann from Israel has a question.

Mr. Federmann: In Israel, we have had great experience for 50 years on how to fight things that were not perceived as a threat yesterday but became so later. This is not police work. You mentioned NATO. Manfred Woerner was a very close friend of mine. Many times, after he became ill, we discussed how we can stop international crime. It is a new modern war against modern society. The police force is very, very important. The whole city of New York would stop if you did not have the traffic police. Here, we must find a way to stop transnational crime. It is the money. We organize all over the world and get bankers to regulate themselves. They do it in Switzerland, and they do it in Germany. Yet, I was in Bonn last week and they told me about $30 billion that went into German banks last year from Russia. In Switzerland, more than $10 billion went into banks in a more or less legal way. We must stop this.

The problem is so great, there is only one central point. No policemen, no FBI, no CIA can stop the dirty money being laundered. Only the banks can do that. We must come to an agreement with all the central banks in the world with a new self-policing organization. I would suggest the name of a man who can do it, to stop this dirty money from becoming clean. This could be done by meetings of 10 people with 10 government banks, and then new regulations could be agreed upon.

Could you go to the central banks of the world and say, let us come to some agreement in order to stop the flow of dirty money? If you could freeze this flow, there would be no money to buy drugs, nor the money to buy arms. Can we do this?

Director Freeh: We do not have that power now. In many of the countries, in fact in all of the countries that we visited, we have neither executive agreements nor mutual legal assistance treaties. This means that, if my investigators or my attorneys need records in a particular central bank in any of those countries, we would really have to rely on the informal processes and the good will of our counterparts over there to retrieve them. So we need, on an international level, the legal wherewithal to get those records.

But more important, as you point out, we need some initiative and some cooperation by the banking institutions. When we did the Pizza Connection in New York, we found out that our drug dealers were taking millions and millions of dollars in suitcases by taxicab down to E.F. Hutton in lower New York City and bringing these valises into counting rooms where tellers sat around and counted up fives and tens and twenties for hours. According to the vice president of E.F. Hutton, when we questioned him later, he was satisfied with the representation of the people bringing the money that this was cigarette money from the Middle East. We need on an unprecedented level the attention and the concern of the international banking community and the financial institutions.

I agree, if we had the cooperation and the authority to access that cooperation, there would be a whole new playing field for us with respect to enforcement. We do not have that, unfortunately, quite yet.

Mr. de Borchgrave: We have a written question that was handed to me: "Mr. Director, did you encounter resistance from extremist nationalist forces in Russia to a greater presence of U.S. police and law enforcement on their soil, and do you expect difficulties on this front?"

Director Freeh: There was, while we were there, and I am sure in the aftermath, criticism by some of the extreme rightist factions in Russia that the presence of two FBI agents in the Moscow embassy was simply a subterfuge for us to conduct espionage and counterintelligence activities. I am sure we are going to find that as we move along, particularly in Russia.

It seems to me, however, that the overwhelming sentiment was to the contrary. The police, the head of the FSK with whom I met, and many of the other intelligence officials were pleased to see law enforcement officers there able to do the things that obviously our intelligence agencies cannot do. This was, in my view, the overwhelming consensus. But, we will get a little bit of that resistance. This is why, at least in that particular role, we have very carefully segregated ourselves from our intelligence agencies because this endeavor is purely a law enforcement one and has to be maintained as one to ensure our credibility and resist this type of criticism.

Mr. Kamen: Jeff Kamen, Fox TV News, Washington.

You told us about Lech Walesa's concerns about nuclear materials possibly being used criminally against the people of Warsaw. What concerns do you have about the potential use for nuclear materials being used criminally against the American people?

Director Freeh: We have grave concerns about that. The Lufthansa flight from Moscow to Munich that carried 10 ounces of highly enriched weapons-grade plutonium could, in our view, have easily been a Lufthansa flight from Moscow or from some other point to Kennedy or Dulles airport. Those materials are not completely in the control of any government, in our view, and I think the growing market, the purchase and sale of those materials, particularly in central Europe, has become quite alarming. It is not a coincidence that we are seeing more and more instances of seizures and interdictions, and we are very gravely concerned about that trend.

Mr. Kamen: If I may follow up, sir, so far as I know—and if you know otherwise, I would be delighted and relieved if you would tell me—there is no firm count available to the Russians or to the Americans as to the exact number or the whereabouts of Soviet SADMs [Special Atomic Demolition Munitions]. Are you convinced that none of these devices—that is to say the explosive elements in them—have been sold to criminal elements?

Director Freeh: I do not know enough of the specifics or facts to answer your question. I do know that there are a wide number of laboratories throughout Eurasia, particularly military weapons laboratories, where both the Russians and not only the Americans but the European nations are concerned about the control of those materials. I think it is a problem that is growing in epic proportions and one that we need to be better prepared to meet.

Question: Mr. Director, can you tell me how your cooperative training efforts have been divided between the local police in Russia, the municipal police, and the federal police?

Director Freeh: The FSK has a vast criminal portfolio including narcotics, terrorism, and nuclear weapons. So we need to work with them. We saw the deputy director of FSK here last week. The director, himself, will probably be over here by the end of the year. We need to set up not just liaison work but probably training with both the FSK and the MVD, and it is going to be a very deliberate and difficult process, but we are moving forward optimistically in that direction.

Question: Mr. Director, I am sure that you have been thinking along the lines of long-term solutions to this problem of nuclear material from the former Soviet Union, but, in the meantime, is there a short-term approach to guard against what we have already seen happen, and that is slippage, a loss of nuclear material via Germany?

Director Freeh: Well, I think there is an immediate reaction and a necessary program on two levels. I think, as we said before, on the G-7 and the summit level it is already being done. I think we have to have our ministries and departments of defense as well as our other instruments of government redouble their efforts and review the physical and electronic security programs we have safeguarding those materials and weapons in both countries.

I think on the law enforcement level what we need to do is do exactly what the BKA police have been doing in Germany. Once we begin to infiltrate the market for nuclear materials in central Europe, which is really a market available to anybody in the world, we will interdict in a most immediate manner the threat that is encroaching now, and that is the vast number of cases—vast, meaning a dozen—where we have corroborated high radioactive materials in a purchase and sale situation. Once we begin making arrests, begin developing informants, and set up the necessary investigative tools, I think you will see a very immediate impact on that market. But, I think it has to be done both from the bottom and the top. And we need the resources to do that.

Claire Sterling: Mr. Director, in the course of tracking organized criminals, for example in Russia, who are dealing in nuclear materials or in other threats to American security, you are bound to run into politicians, members of the establishment certainly at high levels, who will be covering for or working with the criminals. What are your chances? What do you estimate are your chances of getting past problems like the State Department, the White House, the diplomatic corps of our own country and of our allied countries in trying to confront this kind of political problem, which is inseparable from the other?

Director Freeh: Well, as you know, Claire, probably better than anybody in this room, because you have studied it so long and you have written so eloquently about it, we have had this problem before. This is nothing new. We had it in Italy 10 years ago. We have had it in many other countries where we know that a criminal investigation is going to lead to the identification of high-ranking political officials. It really is not uncommon in the history of recent times.

I think what has to be done is two things. One, there has to be on the highest levels—and I am talking about the presidential and G-7 levels—a commitment and a pledge to follow that evidence wherever it goes. If that means we have to take down high government officials in a foreign country or here, then that will be the logical result of that pledge. It is not a problem that, however, should dissuade or obstruct the initiation of what will be the cases perhaps leading to that situation.

I think one of the most important tests of our relationship with the Italian government in terms of assuring each other of our mutual commitment was the evolution of many of those cases that led to the arrest of high-ranking officials and that now, separately in Italy, has led to the arrest of the highest previously elected officials in the government.

I think we have to reach the point—and I will certainly strive to reach that point within my appropriate role—where our counterparts in those countries are as committed to pursuing cases against their ministers or their superiors as they are against the more easily definable criminal elements. That is a position that we have to achieve.

Mr. Stewart: Mr. Director, I am Chip Stewart with Booz, Allen, and Hamilton.

One of the issues that you have alluded to in some of the questions has been how do you watch the universe of what goes on. In the area of narcotics, for example, you talked about a ton getting into the Russia. We talked about our enforcement here and how well it was going, and then we ended up with 21 tons in one seizure, which completely changed the metric. You talked a little bit about money, about how to keep track of money and how that flows.

You had mentioned traditional law enforcement in terms of undercover investigations and the use of informants. Those work extremely well for specific cases. But, if you are going after a whole syndicate or a whole culture that is exchanging money, how do you get the information, and is the Bureau concerned about getting baseline information so they can make a strategic intervention against global organized crime?

Director Freeh: I guess my view of that is twofold. One, I think by working on the right specific cases you achieve the goals that you just alluded to. It may take a little bit of time but, in some ways, that is a more doable strategy than trying to start with the global overview and analysis and penetration of the organization. Judge Giovanni Falcone did not attack the Cupola case in Sicily by opening up an investigation of the 12 heads of the Cupola. We began with the smaller entities, the families, the bosses, and worked our way up. The same strategy was followed very successfully here in the United States. Fifteen years ago, we were not making the cases against John Gotti and Carlo Gambino. We were hitting these very small but powerful gambling operations and loan-sharking operations, and somebody finally said, well, if we make enough of these smaller cases, we can predicate the linkages among them and bring a racketeering case against the larger, more invisible enterprise that is less accessible.

So I think the strategy is a good one. I think we have to start with building blocks. We have to start identifying where our targets are and then finding the legally available ways to bring cases against those targets. That is how you get informants. That is how you get bigger targets. That is how you develop the processes that lead to those cases.

If you look at the universe of the large, powerful syndicates around the world, you are really dealing with a relatively small number of individuals—very, very powerful, very hard to investigate, very hard to apprehend once they have been indicted. I think you start with the building blocks, and I would be willing to follow the successful formula that we followed in the past. I think the targets are different. They may be more difficult in some respects, but they are amenable to the same processes that we have worked before.

Douglas Johnson: Mr. Freeh, I recently had the opportunity to have an extended discussion with the human rights ombudsman of Russia, who was very concerned about the sweeping powers that have been given the police by Yeltsin. He complained, and Yeltsin, in turn, gave him the authority to ensure that those rights were not abused. Of course, he has inadequate resources to do that. I would be very interested in your thoughts on that approach. I suspect it is a necessary approach, but would you see it being replicated in other republics?

Director Freeh: With respect to the emergency decrees, our view of those when we expressed this to the officials that we met with in Russia was that those decrees were ultimately an unsuccessful formula for starting not just a law enforcement process but also guaranteeing a process that would have the support and cooperation of the people.

Ultimately, in the short term, those decrees that do violate various aspects of human rights, although they might prove successful for enforcement, will, in our view and our experience alienate the people who will not be just sitting on juries but providing information and on whose cooperation any good law enforcement depends.

The decrees, however, if we take the president at his word, are temporary measures, in effect, pending the passage of the legislation now in the Duma. All of the officials who have spoken on this have publicly committed themselves to avoiding a repetition of the decrees once those statutes are enacted. The statutes are not yet enacted. They are being held up in the Duma by various political and national interests. So, I agree with the proposition that the decrees are not ideal.

I also think that we have to be realistic about the situation as it develops in Russia. Russia will never be America. America will never be Russia. If you look around the world, even in many of the Western democracies, their systems of constitutional and civil law that have evolved over the years do not mirror our Bill of Rights in many significant ways—even in some of the democracies from which we take our common law and other aspects. So, I think that they will reach a point, hopefully, with our urging, where we can assure ourselves that human rights are being protected along with public safety. But I think that you have to be a realist and not expect that they are going to duplicate everything we have done here in the United States, which, by the way, most countries have not done.

Mr. Webster: Thank you very much, Louis, especially for finding time to respond to the questions, which added to the dimensions of what we heard. I am particularly pleased about the last question because all of us here, I am sure, subscribe to the proposition that any strategy directed toward international and global crime organizations must take into account our adherence to the rule of law, to which, incidentally, Russia has subscribed in its CSCE agreement.

There are several people—and, at the risk of overlooking some, whom I have not yet seen—whose presence I would like to recognize because they are not on the program. We are very pleased to have Senator William Cohen with us this morning, former director of Central Intelligence Dick Helms, former director of Central Intelligence Bill Colby, DEA Administrator Tom Constantine, and former FBI director Bill Sessions.

Global Financial Systems Under Assault: Countering the $500 Billion Conspiracy

William McLucas, Chair
Director of Enforcement, Securities and Exchange
Commission

Mr. de Borchgrave: Ladies and gentlemen, the first panel is "Global Financial Systems Under Assault: Countering the $500 Billion Conspiracy." The $500 billion refers to the latest estimate (from the National Criminal Intelligence Service in England) of the dirty money currently being laundered, which then goes on to buy everything, as we know, from dozens of buildings in downtown Caracas to luxury cruise ships to political parties. I do not think we have to remind this audience that global financial crime threatens to undermine the entire worldwide financial infrastructure.

In the chair for this panel, we have William McLucas, director of the Division of Enforcement at the Securities and Exchange Commission since 1989, whose experience with enforcement at the SEC dates back to 1977.

Senator Patrick Leahy is known to all of us. His vast experience spans 30 years, including 20 years in the Senate, where he has focused on myriad vital issues, on high tech terrorism, and knows how security is increasingly being defined by economic parameters rather than military ones.

Robert Rasor, a 24-year veteran of the U.S. Secret Service is in charge of the Financial Crimes Division, which is responsible for the worldwide oversight, direction, and coordination of criminal investigations that deal with everything from computer fraud to financial institution fraud.

And next is Jack Blum, the internationally renowned attorney and investigator who has played a key role in uncovering the most important international scandals of the past two decades. Few can rival his knowledge in all manner of international financial crime.

William McLucas

I have to give the standard Securities and Exchange Commission disclaimer, which is that my remarks really reflect my own views and do not necessarily reflect those of the commission or any of the individual commissioners—which always leads me to wonder why anyone would want someone from the commission to speak at one of these things.

The issue that we are talking about today, the issue of money laundering and the issue of sanitizing funds that are indeed the proceeds of illicit behavior or organized crime, is a much bigger problem today than it was just a few years ago, as you are all quite well aware. Today, we no longer live in a society where our economy is our economy and that of the European Community or Japan is their economy. We live literally in a global economy today, and that affects not only the banking markets but also the capital markets and the securities markets.

To give you just an idea of the evolution and the globalization of our capital markets, in 1983, the volume of foreign trading in U.S. securities was at approximately $134 billion. By 1993 that volume had reached $617 billion. Likewise, the level of U.S. investment in foreign securities markets in 1983 was at about $16 billion. Today that level is at $555 billion. And one presumes when we use those figures that, generally speaking, we are probably talking about legitimate investment.

The globalization of the markets is indeed a good thing. It provides immense opportunity for investors here. We attract considerably greater capital to our markets than leaves our markets because we are viewed as having the most liquid, the most efficient, and the safest capital markets in the world. The tension that exists is how to facilitate a global market place and a global atmosphere in which capital can move between and among borders relatively freely and yet have in place standards and law enforcement intelligence mechanisms that do not permit or facilitate the laundering or the sanitizing of proceeds of organized crime or other criminal behavior.

In 1992, a Senate report estimated that there was $100 billion annually in money laundering in the United States alone. One can imagine what those estimates are when one talks about the international economy. We will hear more about that, I am sure, from Senator Leahy, who has introduced a bill to deal with counterfeiting and has some proposals that deal with how currency ought to be handled, both on a national and an international level.

I was intrigued by some of the things that Director Freeh said when he talked about the issue of our law enforcement relationship with some of the emerging countries in the former Soviet Union and how we are dealing with, at a law enforcement level, the issue of police on the ground and intelligence gathering.

That is an equally and perhaps more compelling concern when one talks about marketplaces. At the SEC over a period of about 10 or 12 years now, we have negotiated separate agreements—law enforcement understandings—with a couple of dozen countries. We have law enforcement information-sharing arrangements with virtually every developed market in the world, and we are now working to establish information sharing agreements with all the emerging markets. You can imagine the difficulty in the emerging markets of Eastern Europe where the concept of taking rubles from the mattress, walking into an office, handing them over, and getting a piece of paper that says you own shares or bonds in some amorphous entity somewhere is a concept that is not, culturally, very transferable to those markets or those people.

What we are hoping to do through a variety of agreements and technical assistance initiatives is basically to encourage the evolution of markets that, in some respects, resemble our capital markets, where you have not just a disclosure system and a free market concept similar to our markets, but also a law enforcement approach and an approach to compliance that is consistent with what we would view contributing to efficient capital markets.

I probably am not quite as knowledgeable as some of the gentlemen on the panel in terms of the issues that involve cash and cash equivalents. I unfortunately heard Director Freeh refer to the situation where there were tellers sitting in the back room of E.F. Hutton counting the proceeds from the Pizza Connection a few years ago in the Southern District. Generally, in the securities markets, cash is not accepted. There are a number of firms that simply prohibit their offices at the retail level from accepting cash deposits to do transactions.

The concern that we obviously have, however, is with multinational securities firms now. What happens in an office in Caracas or in Asia or in Africa where a customer walks in, in effect, with a bag of money? How do we control the accountability, the reporting, the identity of the customer, and how do we make sure that the concept of compliance that we have in our markets, particularly in the United States with the brokerage industry, get exported to those jurisdictions and by firms doing business there? I am less concerned about that happening in the United States, other than on an episodic basis, than I am in foreign jurisdictions where firms that are not necessarily members of the New York Stock Exchange, or the NASDAQ, set up accounts for the purpose of purchasing and then these accounts come into the system and become part of an account at a member firm, or where the assets are transferred.

We then have the issue, or the possibility, of organized crime figures, people who have gotten their money from drug activity, taking positions in legitimate businesses and owning debt and owning bonds in our capital markets. That is something that the

SEC is working on with the Treasury Department, which is charged with drafting regulations to deal with the issue of reporting and accountability for cash equivalents and where I would expect that over the next year or so we will see developments about what the standards ought to be.

Senator Patrick Leahy

I will try to keep my remarks fairly brief, and I do have a written statement I will put in the record. (Usually we hear other members of the Senate say "I am going to put my full statement in the record." We always assure whoever the senator is that, of course, we will read the record in the morning. I am now 19-and-one-half years behind in reading those records.)

There is a bill that I have sponsored dealing with counterfeiting and money laundering. Mr. McLucas referenced it. It is one that I worked on closely with Dr. Kupperman and others in developing. I did this for a couple of reasons. One, I think we should be bringing our $100 bills up to date and we should have a real impediment to their counterfeiting. I think this is also going to put the squeeze on drug traffickers that have to launder these huge sums of money that have been referred to here.

You take our currency, any denomination, but especially the $100 denomination. Our currency faces the problem of new technologies that make counterfeiting very, very easy. It is no longer like the old movies you saw way back in the black and white days—some little guy in there chipping with an engraving plate. Instead, we're using some very high tech but relatively inexpensive methods to do it. For example, from 1992 to 1993, we found that counterfeit currency abroad, that was detected, had increased by about 300 percent. A number of analysts believe that there is a threat to U.S. security from this counterfeiting. We have credible sources tell us that intelligence experts, both here in the United States and in countries like Israel, are aware of a highly skilled group of counterfeiters operating out of Lebanon's Bekaa Valley, and these counterfeiters appear to be controlled by both Syria and Iran and have turned out as much as $1 billion in very high quality reproductions of the U.S. $100 bill.

Now, notwithstanding our enormous economy, you have to worry about what countries whose interests may well be inimical to ours could do with $1 billion on international markets. These are relatively poor countries. Are they going to use this to buy sophisticated weaponry, thus adding to the destabilization of the region? Will they try to destabilize our currency? I suspect that $1 billion would not do it, but the threat of it and the wide use of it is certainly going to create problems with our currency.

Another possibility that concerns me a great deal, will they use this to fund smaller scale, but still serious, terrorist activities throughout the world? That is an imminent threat to our national security. Think what a terrorist organization, state sponsored and state funded with what appears to be U.S. money, could do in purchasing weapons-grade plutonium, especially today, or chemical or biological weaponry. It is something that our national security people and everybody in this room ought to be concerned about.

We have seen the opening of the Russian republics in the Eastern bloc and how counterfeiting has increased there. According to the chief of the Russian Interior Ministry's Department of Economic Crimes, the amount of U.S. currency confiscated by Russian authorities increased tenfold in one year, between 1992 and 1993. The Moscow news media report that counterfeiting money is a national cottage industry, and, if you have huge inflation in the ruble, something that appears stable like a U.S. $100 bill would encourage counterfeiting.

And last, the problem that is so significant is that our currency is about the easiest in the world to counterfeit. It is certainly the easiest of any *strong* currency. We have updated it with a polyester strip, but our bills do not use the watermarks, the sophisticated dying or engraving techniques or other technologies that other countries employ to make their money very hard to counterfeit. Not only do they make it very hard to counterfeit, they periodically update their currency because that also discourages counterfeiters.

My bill requires the secretary of the treasury to design a new $100 bill with state-of-the-art anticounterfeiting techniques built into it. When we first started talking about this, I was told by Treasury that we cannot really do that because it will create all kinds of problems. Once I introduced the bill, we found that they have already done substantial work on revamping the $100 bill. My legislation intends to make this a reality.

But we also have to realize that the international drug industry is a multibillion dollar industry, as we have heard. There are tremendous problems, and I will not go into them again because we have talked about some of the currency transaction reporting requirements. I have suggested that we have two $100 bills, one in use within the confines of the United States and one used abroad. It would also require bringing in within six months the $100 bills in circulation to get them exchanged for these new notes. That is going to put tremendous burdens on the drug cartels who have hundreds of millions, even billions of dollars, in $100 bills. You have hardship case exceptions, of course, but it would be very difficult for somebody to come in with several suitcases on a flight from Colombia and claim hardship.

The two different versions would allow us to keep track of what comes from abroad. I know that the Federal Reserve likes the current status; they do not like to see changes. It is very comfortable to stay with what you have. It is very uncomfortable for those who deal in such money matters as the Federal Reserve to make changes. But the fact is, we have to. If you talk to some of the DEA money-laundering experts, they will tell you the problems and they will tell me, at least privately, that they are very, very much behind it.

So I would suggest that we have a real discussion, for two reasons, on how we improve our $100 bills to stop counterfeiting. One reason is that I think that we are going to see it used more and more as the currency of choice of terrorist organizations, who find it a very easy way to fund their operations. And second, by doing it, we also have a chance to make a very fast, very effective move against those, especially in organized crime, who deal in huge amounts of $100 bills for money laundering. I think it could be a win-win situation, both for law enforcement and for national security and is something long overdue.

Robert Rasor

Mr. McLucas: We will turn to Robert Rasor, who is the special agent in charge of the Financial Crimes Unit at the Secret Service and who is going to talk a little bit about credit card fraud and telemarketing fraud.

Mr. Rasor: It is becoming more and more clear, whether it is domestic or transnational or international in scope, that financial crimes do not attack individuals, per se, any more. They attack systems. And, of course, the reason that they attack systems is because the money out there has really moved from the banks to systems.

On either a domestic or an international scale, there are a number of things that really need to be looked at. It creates a new dimension for enforcement, as opposed to simply reacting to criminal violations and solving strictly criminal problems, and it is necessary to take a more proactive approach. Because of the nature of what we do and because we are there and we see what is going on, it becomes incumbent on us to be really involved in the risk analysis process. And what that basically does is two things. It gets the criminal off the street, but it also begins to stop the problem from repetitive processes. In a criminal investigation, you do a risk analysis and you apply it to the system. You are really starting to plug the loopholes in the system to stop the repetitive occurrences of the crime. In financial crimes on a global scale, that becomes important because of two things.

It stops the individual from doing it, but it also goes much deeper, because the financial crimes that are occurring are affecting the economy of either the United States or the economy of whatever foreign country it is occurring in, and two things happen in that process.

In a financial crime, of course, there is no taxability to the fraud that occurs, and then that large amount of money at the end of the year in one system or another becomes again a debasement of the tax base. So you really have to start looking at these types of crimes as they are developing and see whether they continuing to cost money to the economies. The Treasury Department and the Secret Service really believe that a fix to the system is as incumbent on law enforcement as catching the bad guy. We have the ability to see what's going on and make some recommendations along those lines.

In the areas with which we deal on a global basis in credit cards and counterfeit currency, we've seen tremendous increases in the overseas activity of these types of things. One that is paramount in the process is that your larger frauds, your larger manipulations, are occurring from counterfeit instruments being produced and presented and accepted as good. Again, that is a system that needs to be looked at. In today's environment, the technology really allows you to produce anything in a counterfeit capacity. Therefore, the economic systems and the financial systems globally and even domestically can no longer rely on sight as a method of authenticity.

You have to go to the backup systems that belong to each and every one of those financial instruments, because there are really adequate backup systems to check and make sure that these instruments, as presented, are genuine. As complex as the frauds become, there is an old adage within the Treasury Department that we repeat time and time again after we do an analysis of these cases and see what made them happen. It comes back to "Know your customer." That is simple. In a complex world, it is not so simple to do, but the way to defeat the process, to get ahead of the technocriminal and the financial crimes expert out there perpetrating major frauds, is for the institutions and the systems to know the customer. And more important than know their own customer, know their own systems.

Time and time again, we look at the problems and we find out that the bad guys, the financial crime organized groups and individuals, hit on a weakness in the system because they know the system better than the keepers of the system. They are able to exploit that and they will continue to exploit that weakness until a system comes in and shuts down the problem.

But what we used to see as loosely associated con men around the world making a lot of money on some frauds has more and more become organized groups that see this as a means to finance their more violent crimes. Most of the money that is taken in major financial crimes, either domestically or globally, does not go to buy the yacht and the house far away any more. It goes back into the business, and the business of most of these people is ultimately violent in nature. So there is a big nexus between financial crimes and violent crimes domestically and worldwide. You are funding violent activities through these processes.

What do you do about that? Well, probably in the analytic process of looking at the activities that have occurred, education is the number one enemy of financial crimes, either counterfeiting or transactional activities. The ability to stop that at the door of the system that has to be used to support that activity is one of the methods of suppressing the problem.

So we are big on education, and we are big on full and complete discussions between the enforcement and the financial communities on what we think they need to do, what they can do, and then getting them to go back into their system, look at their losses, make determinations as to whether those were repetitive in nature, and then help themselves. They have a responsibility as much as enforcement does to know the system that they own, to know where the vulnerabilities are, to stay ahead of the power curve, and to review and fix their systems technologically and systemically.

Enforcement's responsibility, as I have mentioned, is growing into a new dimension, but it also has to be strict enforcement and it has be to basic in nature. I think Director Freeh mentioned success in these basic law enforcement techniques applied to these types of activities. That does work. They are not as sophisticated or as technical in nature as they might be supposed to be.

I think on a global scale the cooperation probably is pretty good. I think Director Freeh's trip to Russia and Moscow and those kinds of things open tremendous opportunities for all of law enforcement, heighten the awareness of the problem, and give our law enforcement the capability to be matched with those of our overseas counterparts.

The Secret Service and the Russian police department have an ongoing process in which there will be some Russian counterparts here helping us on some very significant problems in the credit card area in the northeast, relative to Moscow and the United States.

To be proactive and to suppress the type of activity I am talking about, you have to interrelate with people on a global scale. Those are the things that are going to bring success for enforcement in the future. We will have to look at this with a different point of view, to look at fixing the problem as opposed to just arresting the individuals committing the crimes.

Jack Blum

Mr. McLucas: Jack Blum, who has had substantial experience in the wake of BCCI, and I do not mean that in the pejorative sense, is going to talk about money laundering and some of the problems that are associated with effective law enforcement in the area of international money laundering.

Mr. Blum: In June of this year, working with the BBC TV crew, I took a camera hidden in a briefcase into a bank in the Cayman Islands. I sat with the chairman of the bank and he described for me how to set up offshore in a way in which the U.S.

government could not follow what I did. He went on to explain how I could move money out of the United States by writing checks to corporations he and his bank had set up here in the United States to receive money from people who wanted to hide it.

He described how I could then, through a Caymanian corporation whose ownership was completely concealed, open up brokerage accounts and trade on stock markets anywhere I wanted to. Then finally, he described to me how I could bring money back into the United States without its being traced. Some of the things he told me were really quite astonishing.

For example, one of the things he offered me was a gold Mastercard that I could use that had no name on it. I could put it in the wall anywhere in the United States to get cash, do transactions, make purchases, and there would be no record of whose card it was or of the money for anyone who was looking for it. For example, on the way that I might use it in serious quantity, I said to him, "The gold card won't help me bring money back into the United States if I really want a large amount of money." He said, "Don't worry. We'll move the money that you put in the corporate account in the Caymans to a bank in Europe, which will then lend the money back to you. And when you pay interest to that account, you, of course, will deduct it on your U.S. tax return."

How did I pick this bank? Well, the BBC and I decided we would take the one with the largest ad in the airline magazines enroute to the Caymans. So this was not through some sophisticated tip from criminals.

One of the things Mr. Mathewson, the proprietor of the bank, said is that only fools pay taxes in the United States. And I think he must have had considerable experience. The bank has been around for some time, and it has been around for some time despite the fact that all kinds of information about its problems have been given to the Caymanian bank regulators. Right now, I should not say regulators plural. There is one woman with a high school diploma who is the regulator for 520 commercial banks, including this one. So you get some idea of what is going on there.

What this interview illustrates (an interview that, by the way, you can see portions of on PBS's *Front Line* November 1), is the depth and sophistication of the offshore financial world and the ability to service the needs of drug dealers, thieves or loan artists, con men, securities fraud people, and people who are promoting crime bank fraud and credit card fraud. Now we have two new pieces of business, the fraudulent insurance company that has no assets but sells policies here and the fraudulent and unregulated securities dealers who are selling prime bank instruments that do not exist—in very, very sophisticated schemes.

At the core of this are the anonymous corporations. They are offered in Panama, in the Netherlands Antilles, in Liechtenstein, and in a variety of other jurisdictions where the corporation is owned by whoever physically holds the shares or where the shareholders are nominees. (The nominees are designated nominees through a trust agreement, and it is all set up through a group of lawyers protected by privilege.)

The MLATs (Multilateral Assistance Treaties) we are negotiating are virtually useless against this kind of arrangement for the simple reason that you have to know what you are looking for to get the documents and the materials you need. You have to be psychic to be able to penetrate two or three layers of international corporation where, let us say, the money launderer has a Panamanian corporation. The cash goes into the bank in Panama. It is then transferred through tellers' instruments to a Caymanian corporation or a Netherlands Antilles corporation. You simply can not follow the trail once it disappears in this offshore maze.

Even if you can follow the trail (and occasionally, because of excellent undercover work, people have been able to do it), the difficulty becomes making the case. For prosecutors and police, these cases are absolute nightmares. The evidence comes from several countries. It is probably in several languages. The juries do not have the patience to look at it, and the amount of work relative to the number of prosecutions, convictions, and seizures is just ungodly.

I should tell you that this problem is not a new problem. It began with Meyer Lansky in the casinos in Cuba. Over the years, I have tracked it following people like Robert Vesco, and we have had a series of major fraud scandals in the United States where the money has all disappeared into this offshore world. We have insider-trading fraud money out there and S&L money out there. The problem has exploded. We now have 50 or more tax havens—secret, anonymous corporation jurisdictions [jurisdictions within which corporations can conduct their activities secretly]. Cayman is now up to 520-plus banks. When I first got there in 1974, it was under 100, and there were only six hotels of any size on the island. Now you can get hourly flights from Miami, and they are not using small planes.

The Turks and Caicos and the British Virgin Islands have more than 100,000 anonymous corporations. That ought to be a clue that some things are going on out there that are more than the odd bad-guy transaction.

The focus of law enforcement has been on placement, putting cash in the bank. There are a couple of things about placement that are now completely out of control. One is that Panama once again has become a place where you can bring anything and deposit it in the bank. To me, the solution to this problem is forcing the government of Panama to issue its own currency. No government other than the United States ought to have the U.S. dollar as its currency. That is an invitation to catastrophe and, I believe, a national security threat. We should force the Panamanians to print, issue, and live with their own currency, which they call the balboa but which looks like American currency at the moment.

The second incredible place for this placement of money is now Russia and the former Soviet Union. Money is being shipped there in excess of $100 million a week from legitimate banking institutions. And the reason is that the dollar has become a second currency. From all over the world, criminals are shipping cash to the former Soviet Union and then converting it into legitimate bank accounts by buying commodities, by buying materials that they can then sell in Western Europe and for which they have a legitimate trail. It is a horrendous problem.

But I believe the single worst problem is the British government and its failure to control its own tax havens. They are in the business of renting a flag, renting a foreign service to protect the integrity of these secret corporations. The favored places are the British colonies around the world, whether it is the Channel Islands or the Cayman Islands, because everyone knows that the British flag will guarantee stability. People were afraid of Panama because Noriega could be thrown out. They are not afraid of the Cayman Islands because the crown stands behind it.

We have to do something to force them out of the business, and we can. We are not powerless in this regard. The Fed could tell American banks not to operate there. The Fed could refuse to allow the clearing of wires from tax haven countries in excess of what is reasonably related to the business they do. There are tools. It is a lack of political will and a lack of understanding.

I submit that these are issues that are directly related to our national security. To give you some idea of the dimension of this offshore world, the Cayman Islands are now the fifth largest financial center on the planet in terms of the money that flows through the Caymans. We and the other developed countries of the world are all in deficit. That should come as no surprise because we have a tax hole that gets larger and larger and larger. As this tax hole legitimizes (as people begin to feel, well, it's there, we might as well use it), the hole gets bigger. It has to be closed if we are ever to put our budget in balance.

It also has to be closed to deny the criminals the facilities that they are now using to hide the proceeds of every one of the crimes I have described. If you have any doubt of the dimensions of all of this, just test it. Fly down, look around, talk to people. You will find an incredible industry at work busily protecting and handling and providing an infrastructure to criminals and tax evaders.

Question and Answer Session

Judge Sessions: I was curious about offshore banking operations other than those that you specifically mentioned. Where in other parts of the world do these things take place?

Mr. Blum: Liechtenstein is a favorite place for money paid as bribes to government officials for money laundering. The Mediterranean has a couple of them. We have them in the Channel Islands. We have them in the Pacific—Vanuatu and Nauru. It is a long list and it is easily available. I found that Cyprus is a favorite place for people who are doing business in the former Soviet Union because Cyprus and the countries of the former Soviet Union have gone into various tax treaties and, suddenly, they have boomed as a haven.

Question: Please elaborate on the Russian credit card problem in the northeast.

Mr. Rasor: The significance is that Russian organized crime has been in the United States for some time. One of their pet areas is the credit card area because of the high return. Getting into that type of community is difficult on this side of the fence. The ability to work with Russian counterparts in getting into those systems is what we are looking forward to, and we think we are going to be successful. Is it a big problem with credit cards and Russian organized crime? It is no bigger problem with the Russian organized crime group than it is with any of the other major organized crime groups that are in the United States. The Asians, the West Africans, the inner city gang groups all realize that there is a tremendous amount of profitability in credit card crime.

Mr. de Borchgrave: A question for Senator Leahy. Could you tell us how we plan to bridge that gap between your proposal, which makes eminent sense to this observer, and what Treasury is planning, which, as I understand it, is to phase in a new $100 bill gradually over a period of two years, which would certainly remove any element of surprise.

Senator Leahy: What I intend to do at my level and with my staff is to work with Treasury while Congress is in recess, try to bring us closer together. We did start off poles apart. When I first suggested this, the reaction from Treasury was, well, we just can't change the $100 bill because it would be destabilizing, creating a problem with the float that we now have offshore and so on. Then, when I bring in the legislation, they say, "Oh, yes, we forgot to tell you that there is a proposal under way to change it."

So at least we are coming closer, and I think we have strong support from the various law enforcement agencies in the country, the DEA and so forth. The Secret Service, which has to deal with the question of counterfeiting, has brought up a number of problems.

But the short answer to your question is that we are going to have to work this out, probably not at the debate level on the floor but between the Congress and the administration because, to really work, it has got to be done very fast and with a real time table.

Mr. de Borchgrave: And with a minimum of advance publicity, I assume.

Senator Leahy: And with a minimum of advance publicity.

Ambassador Carol Hallett: Senator, I certainly congratulate you. I think this is something that is long overdue, and I am curious with two questions. First of all, have you considered the possibility of changing the color of the $100 bill that would be used out of the United States? And second, what kind of support are you receiving from the banking community?

Senator Leahy: It is a lot easier to answer the first part of your question. Yes. We would have a different color for the offshore one. This really would not create any problem. Most people when they are traveling do not carry a lot of $100 bills with them. Most tourists do not. Business travelers may. Business travelers either pick up currency here to go abroad or change it, and that would be very easy. They could just simply go to a bank and get whatever number of $100 bills they needed to travel abroad. Every bank here would be able to sell at least an appropriate number of them.

The banking community has expressed some concern to me, as has every numismatic magazine there is. I try to explain to them that they are going to have something new to collect. But it is going to create a great change; it is going to be a lot of extra work. But I do not want to be cavalier and just say, so what. I mean it is going to be a lot more work for everybody if we suddenly start getting flooded with not a billion dollars but two or three or four or five billion dollars in bogus $100 bills, which the Secret Service will say are virtually undetectable. Then what is going to happen? I mean that puts not just that one, two, three, or four billion dollars into question, but that puts into question the hundreds of billions of dollars and the rest of currency that is going back and forth virtually every day. You can imagine what that does. But I think it is high time to do it. They will come around.

Brian Bruh: Jack, from my years in federal law enforcement, I would say you are right on target. What I would also like to add is that Panama itself has offshore banking, as you know, and they also passed a decree four or five years ago through which you can drive a truck, meaning that their regulators really do not regulate. Because of that, I guess I am a little pessimistic, Senator Leahy. I think your efforts there are excellent except in how you think these $100 bills are going to be used against narcotics traffickers. It is so easy to launder money right now that I think by the time we put it into effect, they will be out of cash and into other instruments.

Senator Leahy: That part does concern me a great deal, just as the timing of it and with the intricacies we now see. But it does close one avenue. Then we go after the others. It is not an easy battle. It is not one that we are going to win every time by any means.

Mr. Blum: If I may interject, what the discussion we are having this morning shows is how far behind the curve the U.S. government is and has been. We were taking testimony on container-load shipments of cash going outside of the United

States in 1988 and 1989 in the Senate Foreign Relations Committee. It has taken all of this time to get to the point where we are seriously discussing changing the currency or getting a handle on it. Meanwhile, the sophistication of the people on the other side in terms of handling cash has quadrupled, and the players have gotten better and better at getting around what controls there are.

My sense is that we are a day late and a dollar short always. We have not allocated the kind of money we should have to the project. The big problem at the Bureau of Engraving and Printing is a lack of money. When they started working on the new money, the sample pages were stolen, and that was because there were not enough guards on the job and they were not opening valises. You can't run a government without money. How you can expect to cut through attrition of the staff of Engraving and Printing and then expect them to buy new presses and implement this program is utterly beyond me.

Mr. McLucas: What I find most troubling is that we have international jurisdictions with statutes that issue and establish legal corporations and identities with bearer shares, allowing those entities to transact a series of transfers or fictional business transactions through one or two additional jurisdictions that may at some point surface in a legitimate operating entity with assets. There is very little that people doing business with them—in terms of intelligence-gathering, (applying a "know your customer" role)—can do to make sure that they are not dealing with people who are criminals or who are laundering money.

There are episodic success stories. Years ago when Dennis Levine was apprehended as a result of his insider trading back at Drexel Burnham, that case led to Ivan Boesky, which led to full employment for us for quite a while. Dennis Levine had a bank account in the Bahamas, was operating under an assumed name, and had an arrangement with the employees of the bank there. But through a negotiated agreement with the minister of justice in Nassau, we did get the identity of Dennis Levine.

We currently have an investigation in my office involving tens of millions of dollars that we have been working on for 14 years. I am afraid they will all be dead when we catch them, but we are still pursuing them. It involves insider trading, substantial dollars, and the kind of activity that Jack had alluded to, which is the use of transactions in jurisdictions in which cracking the jurisdiction to get identity of the owners of the entities is basically the problem. We were quite optimistic during the Panamanian crises several years ago. One of the first things we did was contact the State Department to find out what records we could get, because for a period of time we hoped that records from some of the law offices and the banks would be seized. But, as yet, we are still working on the case.

Mr. Blum: The problem, as I see it, is that we have pirate ships in the Caribbean that are actually anchored to sand bars and flying flags that say we've passed blocking statutes. I cannot understand why the United States of America is so afraid of the Cayman Islands. Why should we allow a Caymanian corporation to do business here? They are 18,000 people on a sand bar. I submit to you that you could ask that question about a dozen other places, and we could have a fairly simple standard. That is, if you want to do business here, we have to know who your shareholders are.

The problem is that there are too many quasi-legitimate people—when I say quasi-legitimate, these are business people who set up very sophisticated international tax plans to eliminate American tax liability—who love these places. These include lots of large corporations and wealthy individuals. And when you start talking the way I'm talking, the screams of pain are unbelievable.

I think this is an issue of political will and common sense. We have a genuine national security threat posed by these buccaneer operations. We have the capacity to deal with it through very direct and simple ways, and we are not doing it, and I want to know why.

Question: Mr. Blum, I do not think I heard you mention Switzerland as a money-laundering country although, within the past few years, I think it might have been included on your list. What changed? And if there are things that did change that we could use in the Caribbean countries, what are they?

Mr. Blum: Switzerland gradually began to recognize the tenuousness of its position in the international community by continuing as a buccaneer, and it began to cooperate for the first time, I guess about six or eight years ago, with the SEC and with various other law enforcement agencies in getting after criminals. This is something that has happened over a period of time, and the really criminal money and the fraud artists have moved offshore to other places. Switzerland probably could do more, but very close by, Austria has picked up a lot of the slack. So we have other places and other problems.

Mr. McLucas: If I may add, the cooperation in Switzerland was by opportunity. In the 1980s, during the heyday of the mergers and acquisitions activity in our markets, we witnessed the phenomenon of large trades, primarily in options, being made through the American and the New York Stock Exchanges firms where the customer was an account from a Swiss bank. When options are traded, unlike equities, a settlement can be overnight.

We were successful in getting into court within the 24-hour period to freeze the money in the New York branch of the Swiss bank that had done the options trading. Of course, there was no arrangement with the Swiss and no ability to get the identity of the account owners. The Swiss government's response was that it is prohibited by law from releasing the identity of the account owner to the SEC.

We were fortunate. We had a federal judge in the Southern District who was prepared to look at the reality of the situation and say this simply is not tolerable. We were successful in having $50,000-a-day fines imposed on the Swiss bank until they released the identity of the customer. Within 48 hours, the Swiss government asked us what it was we really wanted to know. That was the beginning of the cooperation, and the memorandum of understanding that we reached means now we are successful in getting information from the Swiss and have a number of other arrangements modeled on that.

That does not work with some of the jurisdictions that you heard referred to here earlier, where the whole raison d'être for establishing an identity there is to avoid disclosure to the United States or to law enforcement authorities.

Giulietto Chiesa: Concerning Russia, the second phase of privatization in Russia is going on already now almost exclusively in cash. There is evidence that in the field of real estate, laundered money is already very largely used.

Mr. Blum spoke of $100 million being imported every week in Russia. According to different valuation in Russia, there probably is 10 times that–$1 billion. Laundering money in Russia is incomparably easier than elsewhere in the world–a country without borders, without police, without controls, with an extremely high level of corruption reaching to the political summit of the country. In the short term, we are witnessing the criminalization of an entire political elite. The next election in Russia will be financed by this dirty money.

The question, it seems to me, is very urgent, and what Mr. Blum said this morning about this question being a security problem for the West is all too evident. Russia in the next 10 years will be a very strong and very rich country. That means that the discussion is not only strategic but also has a tactical content. My question then is, do you think it is possible to intervene directly and in the very short term to face this danger?

Mr. Rasor: I will start with that. I think the problem that you pointed to is somewhat accurate. I think the solutions have already begun. With Director Freeh's trip to Russia this summer and the dialogues that have started to develop there between American and Russian enforcement officials and some other entities, the process has already begun. There is a unique opportunity in that process because, as you described it, it is pretty random at this point because there are no systems. Systems need to be developed. But we have a great opportunity to help develop systems knowing what we know already about the fraud problem. So although the problem is going to continue, steps have been taken in the right direction. The knowledge in the United States about financial crimes and problems and all those attendant systems enables us to help develop those Russian systems. That will be extremely helpful.

Senator Leahy: A couple of weeks ago, in anticipation of President Yeltsin's visit here, I went to Russia and brought a small group of senators. Our discussions showed that the problems are not going to be solved just with the summit meetings between President Yeltsin and President Clinton. But I think what is probably important for these summit meetings is that a whole lot of people at other levels start working on mutual problems. This is one of the things that is being discussed both with some in the Russian government and with people ranging from our financial experts to our law enforcement people. I think it is important. They say the dollar is the de facto currency in Russia, and several days there proved it. With everything from shopping to hotel bills to restaurants, I did not even spend my $40 or $50 in rubles because I just spent dollars. I mean everywhere on everything—from street vendors to restaurants. And I realize what this means, but I believe that is being discussed this week. We still have a long way to go.

Mr. Blum: I wanted to add that I am extremely pessimistic about solving this problem. I have been having conversations with a senior official in the Moscow police department. And what they tell me is, how do you go after financial crime when you have police officials who do not understand what a bank is in a Western sense? Remember, these are senior people who have never experienced capitalism and the various forms and financial instruments, and here are fraud artists who are light years ahead of some of the most sophisticated police in the world. They are going in and dealing with what have to be our equivalent of country bumpkins who simply do not know what they are dealing with.

Mr. McLucas: Part of the problem, I think, is going to be that we have to literally export not just an ethic but a concept of a market as a way of doing business. That is culturally perhaps as big a problem as the entire law enforcement problem.

Claire Sterling: I think there is a very serious danger of self-delusion here if we think that establishing an FBI office in Moscow, which does not yet have its first agent in place, will come anywhere near approaching the dimensions of this problem. It is not just a technical or a financial problem or a problem for the SEC or the Secret Service. It is a political problem of immense dimensions that has to be addressed by the White House, the National Security Council, the State Department, and all of our allies, who should not be forgotten for their very serious guilt in this connection when Mr. Chiesa has pointed out that privatization in the second stage in the Soviet Union is now being dealt with in cash. If we do not address this question at the highest political level, we are lost. We might as well forget about the rest of this conversation.

Mr. McLucas: Claire, I am glad you have exonerated the SEC from that responsibility.

Mr. Blum: A question passed to me asks, can you discuss the electronic transfer problem? Well, the problem that electronic transfers have created is the speed with which people can hide things. We can now watch money disappear instantaneously and, in the space of one day, transit 5, 6, 7, 10 jurisdictions and any number of corporate shells, so that the speed has made tracing efforts a very, very difficult thing indeed.

Now, there have been discussions about regulating electronic transfers. It is a very complex thing to do. We are talking about $1 trillion a day clearing New York alone, and every time you come up with some idea about how to do it, the bankers and the people who run the system tell you, you're going to make us crash and you do not want to do that.

I offer this though as food for thought. About 1960, I am told, the ratio of financial transactions internationally to goods and services moving internationally was about two-and-one-half to one. Today, for every dollar in goods and services, it runs about nine-and-one-half to one. Now, that ought to tell you a little something about what is going on in the world economy and let you puzzle a bit over why we have to have all of these financial transactions in ratio to trade. It just does not make clear sense.

Question: If I may take a shot at a short-term solution—just partially, though, because I am also not too optimistic right now about the ability of law enforcement from the Soviet Union to do something. Bankers have been slain in Moscow in the dozens in the past few years. The bankers, or all financial people are actually the first line of defense, and there is no way to get bankers or other financial people to cooperate with their government unless their government is not only honest but can protect them.

And so, in my judgment, one of the things that our law enforcement should be working on also is trying to figure out ways to protect the financial community, to educate the financial community, and to get the financial community to work with their own law enforcement, which they generally look down upon, and for good reason.

I just want to follow up on a question. I think Jack Blum mentioned the "wired" world. How can we use technology to fight organized crime or international organized crime? I think we are all making very good points about how organized criminals have used technology against us, particularly when you mention the "wired" world. Is there any way we can use some of the technologies from even the security agencies, the defense agencies, or whatever? I am thinking in terms of artificial intelligence, because as soon as you get into the "wired" world (and that is where everybody is trying to turn all of his cash, whether it's greenbacks or whatever color it is), the cash is lost to law enforcement unless you know what you are looking for. So, I wonder if anyone on the panel can talk about how we can use the new technologies that we have now to fight organized crime?

Mr. McLucas: Well, I guess I will start with that. We do it to a great extent already. We can track every security that crosses the New York Stock Exchange on a daily basis to an account—the time that the order came in, the time the trade was executed.

The problems, as you have heard, go a little bit beyond that. Even in this country, remember, concepts of privacy are held near and dear by all the people who also listen to what you heard discussed today and are appalled that drug lords can take advantage of our markets and launder money. So I do not think the balance is that easily struck. The technology is there. I think the issue is probably more an international policy issue. If we simply had a level playing field, even with our concepts of privacy and the right to financial privacy and things like that, our law enforcement system would operate effectively. My belief is that it is not a technological problem; it is a policy problem.

Mr. Blum: I very much agree. It is not a technology problem. I can incorporate you in the Cayman Islands for $1,500. For another $1,500 I can make it totally anonymous, and for another $1,000 I can maintain the corporation for at least a year. That low-cost facility enables criminals to use these corporations for one deal, one transaction. And by the time you have gotten the name of the corporation in the database, the transaction is over and the money is gone. So I do not see what the technology will do until and unless you destroy the ability to set up these corporations up anonymously.

Mr. Rasor: I would just add a little, and probably Brian Bruh could tell us more what FinCEN is doing in that regard. But one of the things that can be done and is being done in this process (although none of these things are going to solve it, but will just reduce the odds and reduce the ability for these things to continue) is the analysis of information through such agencies as FinCEN (the Financial Crimes Enforcement Network), which takes that data, collects it, analyzes it, and projects continuing problems.

So you are using your technology, you are using the trail that is left after the crime has been committed to build for future activities. Analyzing what happened in the past and trying to prevent it in the future does occur and does continue.

One other side note on that. The most effective way to do that is internally—the systems themselves and the people that are in those systems can tell you quicker than anybody else what's going on.

Question: When money comes in from abroad through entering an account, the bank accepts it. Most of the banks do not ask who is behind this transfer. You cannot come in with $100,000 or $200,000 in cash, but once you send money from the island to another island via Zurich, Zurich accepts it under the law. You must have legislation in Europe that stipulates that before the money is accepted, the account must have a name or a company. Then, under the name and under the company, you can control the receiver of the money. This is a way we may improve the picture. But in Europe, every bank accepts money that comes from another bank, and this is the greatest business today in Europe. Many things have been established in Zurich and around Zurich for this very purpose.

I own a small bank in Zurich. We had in the last two months, through a very reliable person, an offer for five times the value of the bank for sales to some Russian puppets. I think this is where you should focus your attention and your legislation.

Mr. Blum: If I can expand on that a bit, a number of banks now offer the use of their names and their accounts in other banks. So we have a phenomenon called "payable through." In other words, if you have a bank in Panama that sets a deal with a bank in Miami, you can receive interchangeable checks, with the name of either bank on the check itself.

The second piece of business that is going on is on account opened on behalf of, let us say, a Panamanian bank branch located in Zurich. The modus operandi is rather simple, the money gets deposited to the branch, and it looks like a transfer to the bank, but, in reality, it remains with the individuals. This is also very difficult to penetrate and is on the list of things that I think ought to be prohibited.

Mr. Stewart: The contrast on this panel is really striking, at least to me, and that is that Mr. McLucas and Senator Leahy and Robert Rasor from the Secret Service are talking to us about problems that are manageable and that we are sort of moving toward solving. I felt very comfortable when Senator Leahy was talking because your bill is very good, and the SEC is the control, and the Secret Service says these are ordinary criminals that are fundamentally no different than street thugs, and we have them pretty well under control if we take it a case at a time.

Then I heard Mr. "Gloom" Blum, who said, my God, these are sophisticated people, and it is not the wire transfer that is the problem because that is easy to deal with. The problem is the enormous amounts of cash that are passing through hands in legitimate ways all over these countries that we have sort of neglected. We went to wire transfers, but nobody paid attention to this cash that is just flowing like mad in legitimate channels, which causes all kinds of problems.

My question to the panel is, is this, in fact, not very much of a problem, or has it been underfunded, unattended to, and underappreciated so that it slipped below the threshold of our radar out there that is looking for the one case where the informer calls us up, so we can work that case back rather than taking a look at the larger picture?

Senator Leahy: My first decade in public life was as a prosecutor, and I must admit that I take more of a law enforcement view on this. I feel that in many of these areas, especially areas of sophisticated crime, it is underfunded and underappreciated. I think that sometimes the idea of law enforcement in the Congress is simply that we will just increase the penalties on everything and we'll give the death penalty for everything from aggravated jay walking on up.

The fact of the matter is that it does not do a damn thing for law enforcement. I once had a legislator tell me when I was a state prosecutor, well, look at all this trouble with armed robberies. We're going to double the penalty for armed robbery. I said, "whoop-de-do." Nobody commits a robbery unless they think they are not going to get caught. They do not care what the penalty is because they assume they are not going to get caught. It is like having two warehouses side by side, one with security and alarm systems, one without. You know which one gets broken into.

The problem here is that we have not put in the security systems, we have not put in the alarms, and there is nothing that is going to slow this down better than some very good, effective prosecutions of people who today assume they will never be caught and they will never be prosecuted. We could have all the laws in the books, but if people assume they are not going to get caught, what difference does it make? You do not speed on the interstate in an area where you know they always run radar. Well, you may be the only person who has never sped. If you are like some of the rest of us, you probably speed on those roads where you know nobody ever patrols. We are not patrolling some of these areas.

Mr. Blum: I think part of this problem is a little bit different than what we have been talking about. The underfunding and the failure to put money into systems is real. But there is something else at stake here. Law is normative. We all understand that the reason law works that is most people obey it. A professor of criminology who taught me years ago always said there is a dark side of crime. All the police ever get are the 10 percent of the least competent criminals and that really what you are looking at in criminal law is enough enforcement to keep the problem from getting out of control. But if people do not believe in the law and think it is a joke, no amount of law enforcement will stop them.

Now, what we have developed is a kind of normative feeling about how to operate internationally and that is you can move offshore, you can hide your assets from a lawsuit if you are a doctor by setting up a trust in the Cayman Islands, or for tax evasion purposes. I had one guy who wanted to get a divorce who walked into my office and said, my wife has hired three great white sharks, can you help me hide my money? When you get the average person saying I can opt out of the laws and regulations of my country, particularly the tax laws, it then becomes so much easier for the financial structure to defend the mechanisms, for people to go on about their business and say, well, this is just silly government regulation. I think it is that attitude that has to be cracked, particularly in the international banking community and the international taxation community. I think that is where the answer to this problem begins.

CHAPTER 3

"Hacking" through the Cyberspace Jungle

L. Dain Gary, Chair
Manager, Computer Emergency Response Team

Mr. de Borchgrave: This panel, as you know, is called "'Hacking' Through the Cyberspace Jungle." What does that mean? It means that tomorrow's villain or despot armed with a computer and a small squad of expert hackers can be as dangerous and as disruptive as the adversaries we have faced in the past.

Given the fact that global information systems are only as secure as the weakest link in an interconnected global system, the potential for corruption and compromise of financial and national security and law enforcement networks is already with us. Telecommunications and computer systems are being exploited by illegitimate businesses and criminal organizations, and the list of financial targets continues to grow with enhanced system compatibility.

Chairing this next panel is Dain Gary, who manages the Computer Emergency Response Team's Coordination Center located at Carnegie Melon University's Software Engineering Institute. This means that he is as good as they come in his field, a computer genius who has spent four years at the National Computer Security Center.

Donn Parker has written five books on computer crime and information security and has spent 24 years on computer security at SRI. A world-renowned expert, Donn is the recipient of the 1994 National Computer System Security Award.

Scott Charney is chief of the Computer Crime Unit at the Department of Justice and has been dealing with high tech crime in one capacity or another for 14 years. He is the gentleman tasked with implementing the Justice Department's Computer Crime Initiative, and he has five federal prosecutors on his staff.

Special Agent James Christy is director of Computer Crime Investigations at the U.S. Air Force's Office of Special Investigations, the wizard who was the original case officer in the Hanover Hacker Affair. The case involved a group of German hackers who electronically penetrated the Defense Department's computer systems all over the world and sold the extracted information to the Soviet KGB. Jim's work was detailed in the best seller, "The Cuckoo's Egg," which spawned a PBS docudrama. The

Federal Computer Investigations Committee, known as FCIC, comprises computer crime investigators from almost every federal agency, and Jim was its vice chairman for four years.

So, Dain Gary, beam us up into cyberspace and tell us whether you see a Three Mile Island or perhaps even a Chernobyl in the world of information systems.

L. Dain Gary

I thank you for that glowing introduction. I am delighted to be here this morning. As we sat and listened to the very interesting comments by the previous panelists, I was quite pleased and interested to see that at the close of the last session we began talking about high tech and the electronic medium. It is not only interesting but necessary for us to understand the currency issues. I fully appreciate that. It is a little bit apart from the world that we live and work in right now.

Director Freeh, in talking this morning about the work they have been doing in the FBI to improve relations and improve the training of investigative and law enforcement agencies worldwide, mentioned very fundamental issues of investigative tactics, techniques, undercover agents.

I am here to tell you that the law enforcement agencies worldwide are considerably behind your adversary in the area of electronic warfare, information warfare. We can talk about currency exchange. We can talk about offshore banks, but each of you well understands that the transactions are electronic. All of the information that we are talking about today, whether it is currency, whether it is corporate proprietary design issues, whether it is merger issues, whether it is political strategy, has all been reduced to an electronic format as available in the systems that we are using today. Those systems have not been made secure.

It is one of the things that we want to talk about this morning to raise your awareness a little bit as to the vulnerabilities that exist in these systems.

I do not know how many of you are aware of the CERT Project in Pittsburgh. The CERT, the Computer Emergency Response Team, was founded in 1988 by ARPA, the Advance Research Projects Agency, as a direct result of the Internet Worm Incident. To give you an explanation, the Internet is that large network that couples all the research and universities together, supercomputer centers, and so forth of interest to ARPA and the research community. That particular incident disabled some 6,000 sites in the network. That was 1988.

Since 1988, CERT has been operating at the Software Engineering Institute in Pittsburgh. We have grown now to 14 members of the technical staff. The number of incidents we handle has grown from 132 for all of 1990 to an average of 195 per month in 1994—computer intrusions and incidents in the Internet, that is.

The Internet has grown by 3,000 percent since that time, but there are other response teams in the fray. There are now 33 other incident response teams organized and located around the world. There are seven in Europe. There is one on the Pacific Rim in Australia. So, although our team is seeing an increase of 77 percent per year in computer intrusions in this network community, there are now 33 other teams that are assisting in this work.

The problem is staggering. I cannot give you the magnitude of the loss. I cannot measure that for you. One of the things that Donn will do this morning is talk to you a little bit about the people that are involved.

CERT provides a forensic service. We are interested in the technologies that are at issue. How was the system compromised, and what can we do to prevent subsequent compromises? This is all very, very reactive, as you can imagine.

In February of this year we issued a press release. (It is the first ever. We normally maintain a fairly low profile.) We issued the press release because a situation had developed in the network we felt we were compelled to say something about publicly, the introduction of what we are calling "snippers" into the network. Basically, after that date reusable passwords in open systems became obsolete. You can no longer use the same password repeatedly as you are logging in to a distant system through the network. The "snippers" are out there. They are grabbing passwords. They are grabbing log-in IDs. They are grabbing account data. And that information is then replayed against the distant account and, to that system, you look like a legitimate user.

There was some discussion about the records that are available, the audit trail that is available to allow you to track a transaction back to an account or an individual—assuming that the account and log-in and audit data are available to you. The intruder is very sophisticated, and, guess what, the first thing they try to do is to try to alter that log file. If they gain control of the system, they can manipulate the audit records in such a way that you do not have a clue as to what is going on in that system.

The numbers are staggering. Our folks are working 12 hours a day. We are operating seven days a week and have a 24-hour hotline. But the problem that we see is one of lack of understanding and awareness and a lack of training and technical competence on the part of the user community. The technology, the software is changing every 12 to 18 months, the hardware every 36 to 48 months. And we are not keeping abreast of it. The operators are not, to say nothing about the law enforcement agencies and the regulatory agencies. We are finding that every year there is a freshman class that comes into the Internet, and every year that freshman class makes the classic mistakes. I can show you slides of five of the top penetration practices, and the vulnerabilities being used have been documented for five years. They are still being successfully used.

The Internet is a huge laboratory, and there is a lot of experimentation being done. The work that is perfected in the Internet is then imported into proprietary networks. (The technologies, you understand, are all the same.) So, if you learn how to compromise systems in the Internet, you can take that expertise, those techniques, those tools into any corporate network environment, any proprietary environment, anywhere on the planet and be successful. The tool kits are available in the network. It has only taken a handful of smart people to compromise these systems. They will document those techniques and they will package the tools necessary to do it and make them available in the community. So you have a lot of "wanna-bes," you have a lot of copycats that are out there compromising these systems.

I do have just a couple of slides I would like to show you. What we are seeing in what I will call on intrusion profile is a much more complex and much more technically sophisticated intruder—automated tools, automated attacks, very, very calculating. They know how to exploit protocol flaws. They have source files for the systems that you are using, and they are exploring that source file to find vulnerabilities that we do not know about.

Regarding various types of incidents, there is no formula for what happens once this individual or these individuals are inside the system. The attack techniques are very similar. We know how they attack the systems. We issue advisories to the community. One hundred and twenty-two advisories have been issued by CERT to date detailing the problems in the systems and detailing how to correct those deficiencies.

The problem that we have is that we do not have any enforcement capability, and so it is left to the end-user to decide that the risk is great enough to invest in needed security countermeasures. That decision has not been made by most organizations yet and usually is not until after an intrusion has occurred.

You hear people talk about how to improve security. I will tell you how to increase your problem. If you will run down this list, and if you can relate to any of these, then you are basically enhancing the problem in your organization. Generally we find that management will deny the problem: This is not a problem for us; this has never happened here; we do not have this problem. That is probably a true statement. It is absolutely the fact, but the other fact is that you are not operating now as you have operated in the past. You are more vulnerable. You are more exposed: no policies or direct Internet connection without a firewall or gateway or filtering routers.

This is probably the most significant problem of all. The people operating your systems do not understand the technology that they are using. Right now, we do not have any way to prevent this activity. We can make recommendations. We can make suggestions. We can offer solutions. Whether they apply to the systems remains to be seen, and it is ultimately an individual decision. The corporate managers must take responsibility for security in the systems. Information, as we talked about before, runs the full gamut of corporate America, whether it is human resource information, whether it is the on-line catalogue. Someone has got to take responsibility for that information. It is currently not being done. It is currently someone else's job in the organization. Whether that is the application designer or the network administrator, it is someone else's job. And too much of the information is being withheld. We have a difficult time—and I understand it completely–in having organizations tell us of the impact of the intrusion.

CERT, if it has any reputation at all, has built it on trust. We do not disclose information about site-specific activities. If we are dealing with 195 incidents per month, that is 195 sites that have confided in us and asked us to help them solve their problem, knowing that we will not tell law enforcement, we will not tell the Securities Exchange Commission, we will not tattle. Basically we are there to help them solve the technical issues. We work closely with the law enforcement organizations. We work closely with everyone else in the community, but we hold dear and we hold sacred the site-specific information that is reported to us.

But in too many communities, there is no information being disclosed. Therefore, you do not get a real sense of the problem. I can only stand here and tell you we are seeing a 73 percent increase per year, and numerically, that is going to touch you very, very quickly.

I would like Donn Parker to step up now and talk a little bit about the survey that they have done focusing on the individuals who are on the other side of this phenomenon.

Donn Parker

Some people know me just as the bald eagle of computer crime. At least there are a lot of hackers who know me that way. I am going to base my remarks on a two-year study we completed earlier this year on the vulnerabilities of our public switch telephone systems to hacker attacks, software hacker attacks.

We interviewed about 80 malicious hackers in Europe and in the United States. We find ourselves in a very unusual situation. This is a leap in the level of abstraction from the first panel to the second panel—the idea that mature adults are sitting around talking about what a bunch of juveniles going through puberty are engaged in. Information is the commodity of crime, and before any of the money laundering, before any of the transactions take place, it is a matter of the movement of information. And the Internet, as Dain now has emphasized, is causing on explosion in the means of moving that information, and the use of cryptographic protection of the information is another growing and serious problem that we must deal with.

So, as Stewart Brand said, we are in the golden age between warning and disaster as far as new threats to our country and internationally through the very rapid movement of information.

To start with the overall problem of losses in the business world, we are concerned here with the same old crimes that we have always been concerned with: fraud, theft, larceny, embezzlement, sabotage, espionage, extortion, conspiracy. And, as we are starting to see in the news media, we are faced with business losses in a variety of new ways with the automation process and the Internet means of communication as a critical factor. So, they are the same old crimes seen in an entirely new environment that has changed the nature of business losses.

Today, we are dealing with new kinds of criminals-high school students going through puberty. And we are dealing with new environments, the electronic environment that we hear all about: the problems of shoulder surfing, of boxing, of Trojan horse attacks, computer viruses, software piracy, and so on. Again, a bunch of terms that you have read about, I am sure, in the news media.

The forms of assets have certainly changed dramatically, because we are now dealing with electronic money. I have interviewed over 200 so-called computer criminals and, in studying these business crimes and the movement of money, I find that criminals now have a new problem. And this new problem is, how much money should I steal or how much money should I move? It does not matter any more how much money. Once you get the money into electronic form, it is only where you put the decimal point. And, in interviewing career criminals, embezzlers within large companies, what we find is that, if they try to steal too much money, they will be caught. I mean it is just inevitable that, if you steal too much money through a legitimate business operation, the victim must catch you. You must be caught, which you will be for very large transfers of money.

We also found that if you do not take enough money you are going to be caught, because you do not have enough money to hire a good lawyer and accountant and travel well to stay free. It is easy to catch people stealing small amounts of money. It is easy to catch people stealing very large amounts of money. We had a 70 million Swiss francs funds transfer from London to Zurich; the individual was caught because he tried to take too much money at one time. It is noticed. People notice a large amount of money and question it.

So the average funds transfer today is in the range of $23 million dollars. And, as long as you stay in the round-off error of $23 million, you are perfectly safe in the amount of money you can move very rapidly around the world.

Now, how do you have this leap of abstraction from these kinds of people from the organized global criminals that we talked about to the juveniles? The juveniles possess the technological capabilities that the large-scale criminals need in order to move their information, communicate, and, in fact, move their electronic money, and therein lies this leap from large-scale criminal activity to juveniles.

Now, I am going to talk about the solutions—just based on the studies that we have been doing. There are three legs to the stool that provides those solutions. First is the INFOSEC, or the information security aspects. This is a critical part of security, of having a strong, locked door electronically. And the way to achieve that is through the alertness of the management people responsible for providing the money, the budgets, and the impetus to provide the fire walls and so on—the technological controls that Dain talked about.

Second, a critical factor in the technological aspect is now becoming the use of cryptography, scrambling information using secret keys. This is a critical factor because we are currently headed toward what is known as absolute privacy (that is, the use of strong crypto that cannot be decrypted in wire taps, in eavesdropping by our criminal justice community). This is a critical factor because there are many people opposed to providing law enforcement with the technological capability they need to decrypt this encrypted information.

We are headed in our business organizations into what I call "information anarchy," where this powerful control of encryption can be used by employees to take control of the assets of the corporation away from the management, the people who are accountable for those information assets, by simply encrypting them using strong crypto. On this basis, we go to the second level of concern here of controlling the problem through the law. I believe we need a new law that would make the use of strong crypto in the furtherance of a crime a crime. What I am talking about is the difference, for example, between robbery and the more serious crime of armed robbery. We need a law that will change ordinary criminal activity to a more serious level of criminal activity if strong cryptography is used. We must find a means of controlling that strong cryptography.

There is a new experiment that I claim is the information security experiment of the 1990s conducted primarily by the NSA and that is the use of escrowed secret keys under the control of government agencies. This is absolutely necessary to eliminate what I call absolute privacy. We must eliminate absolute privacy or our own privacy is going to be destroyed, because it will allow criminals to engage in their communication of information, and they will not be touchable by law enforcement. We must control the use of strong crypto if we are going to deal on a level playing field with the criminal elements in society.

Finally, the third point from the study that we did of malicious hackers: these young high school people in and of themselves may not be particularly dangerous directly. They remain a tapable resource by real, adult criminals, however, because they possess the technological capabilities the real criminals need to communicate their information and their electronic money.

The way to solve that problem, I believe, is through an interdiction program in which we can stop young people (9, 10, and 11-year-old children) from going into the dead-end hacker culture. Once they are in that culture, we have lost them, because they have become addicted. Just like an addiction to drugs, they are addicted to their hacking culture. We find many of the hackers, however, once they are in the culture, will leave that culture when they are 18- to 24-years-old. Now, of course, the ones who stay in it and go into adult criminal activities are going to be doubly dangerous, having the technological capability and the means and motivation for large scale crime.

But many of these young people are going to drop out, and we can reduce the hacker culture—the number of children in that hacker culture—if we can stop them from going in from the beginning. This means working through YMCAs, through PTAs, through teachers in grammar school. I know it is hard to imagine that, on one hand, we are talking about global organized crime and, on the other hand, we are trying to get science teachers in the seventh grade to deter young people from using this very powerful technology in the hacker culture. It is hard to imagine this leap in the level that we need to consider. Nonetheless, we must get to the game producers who can distribute deterrent leaflets, and we must get into the games that are distributed to our young people, and we must convince them that they are learning a powerful new technology that can be used to greatly damage our society.

Scott Charney

Mr. Gary: I would like to ask Scott Charney to address the group. Scott, as you recall, is the chief of the Computer Crime Unit at the Department of Justice and their initiative is the Computer Crime Initiative. Donn was talking about laws, some of the requirements and the needs, and Scott can fill in some of that information.

Mr. Charney: It is really interesting how this technology is affecting us broadly as a society. You know, listening to Donn's comments about these young kids who get into the hacker culture, everyone has to understand that this new technology, this revolution, is different than prior revolutions. These kids are using a technology that their parents and teachers do not understand. When automobiles were invented, adults drove first and then they taught their kids how to drive. In this technology, the kids are the first ones behind the wheel.

In investigating hacker cases for the Justice Department, we very often find that we have a hacker breaking into government systems, and we go to the hacker's home and we talk to the parents and we say, "You know, your kid is upstairs breaking into federal systems and if he does not stop, he is going to be arrested." They are shocked. They think (1) it is great he has a hobby; (2) it is high tech, he will be able to get a job; and (3) he is not on the street using drugs. All true. But he is still committing crimes. And when we say to them, he is using the Internet, they do not know what that is. So we are really in the midst of a revolution. And the first question is, how bad is the problem? Everybody wants to know. The answer is no one knows, and there are two reasons for that.

First of all, no one has agreed on an acceptable definition of computer crime. If you go to a pay phone here in the hall and I engage in shoulder surfing, I walk behind you and I watch you enter your pin number. I write it down, and then I make a long distance call and I charge it to you. When I enter your number, it is checked by a computer. Is that a computer crime? If that's a computer crime, take your statistics and add about $2 billion a year, because that is what the major carriers say they lose to toll fraud. If you just call it toll fraud and not computer crime, you come up with totally different statistics.

The second thing is that there is no centralized reporting. In trying to get a handle on how bad the problem is, I have looked in the newspapers. And what do they say? They quote experts as saying that computer crime is costing the United States between $500 million and $5 billion a year. I actually saw one report in the *Washington Post* that said $500 billion. I assume it was a typo. The Internet attacks that Dain talked about, though, are an indication of where we are going. The number of attacks is on the rise and the attacks are getting more serious. (In a second, I will talk about the changing face of computer crime.)

You also need to realize that IDSs (intrusion detection systems) will redefine the problem. IDSs have gone under many different names. Basically what we are talking about is using the computer to look for anomalies to tell us that here is something that is different that you should look at, that human beings usually do not catch. Let me give you an example.

You could set up a program in the Justice Department that keeps track of when I sign on in the morning and when I sign off at night. So they would say that every morning Charney signs on sometime between 9:00 and 9:30. Then one day Charney signs on at 8:00. The computer says he is out of his pattern, and a system administrator is notified. The system administrator calls my office. I am not there. They call me at home. I say, I just woke up. I am not on-line; they now know they have an intrusion.

Why is IDS so important? Because, when the air force tested the network security monitor at the University of California at Davis, they found that computers are far better at tracking intrusions than humans. The increase was about 300 percent. The problem is, if you are getting that many reports of problems, what do you do with that much information? It sometimes takes months to track down one isolated intrusion or one series of intrusions. How are you going to track hundreds? Who is going to investigate them? I should also point out that the problem is going to get worse because of what I call the "Charney Principle," which is this: there is always a percentage of the population up to no good. Fortunately for us, the law-abiding people, that percentage is small. Right now, however, you have a percentage of people up to no good, and most of them are not computer literate. Twenty to thirty years from now, they will all be computer literate. They will all recognize how you can abuse this technology and things like the Internet that give you anonymous FTP (File Transfer Protocol). You know, there are groups that like anonymity. People interested in protecting their privacy are one group. Criminals are another group. And this technology is great for engaging in anonymous communications, anonymous acts from faraway places, long-distance.

Now, I said the face of computer crime is changing, and that is true. Let me tell you what we have seen in the last three or four years since the department has been working on the Computer Crime Initiative. First, we used to deal a lot with young hackers and the teenagers. No more. They are now in their twenties and thirties. The crowd is getting older.

Second, their motives have changed. It used to be that a lot of these people were merely curious about computer systems and networks. They were exploring, but they had what they called the hacker ethic. They meant no harm; they just wanted to learn. That is not true any more either. They now have recognized as they get older that they need a source of income, that they need profit. Information is something you can sell, and, if you look at the way computers have been implemented and integrated into our societal fabric, you can see that this is a great opportunity. Why? Because in the old days, when we had sensitive information, we put it in a locked file cabinet. We locked the office door. We locked the building. We put a fence around the building, and we had guards walking around.

Then we went to networks. We took the information out of the safe, put it in a network, and all rested easy because we had a fence around the building. That fence does not work any more, and that information is all available. And, as the hackers have begun to realize this, they have recognized that there are a lot of reasons they should be interested in that information, for example, in the phone companies. The telephone system is one huge computer network. It did not take the hackers long to figure out that they could access the phone company's computers and look for PIN registers on their own phones and the phones of their friends. They could look for wire taps. They could do this at very little risk and find out who we were investigating and whether they were under investigation. Sometimes it even works the other way and helps us. There was one hacker we managed to identify in part because every time he left the phone company's computer he looked for a PIN register on his mother's phone.

But the truth of the matter is, as more sophisticated criminals in the organized crime community recognize that you can either do it yourself or—for a small amount— you can pay a hacker to see if there is a PIN register on your phone, a track and trace device on your phone, or a wire tap on your phone, they are going to do it, and it is a big problem for law enforcement.

Indeed, we had one case involving the Legion of Doom in Atlanta, where the hackers actually went into the Federal Building into the phone closet and tracked all the lines of the Secret Service. This is not a theoretical threat.

The other thing that everyone has to recognize is that this whole new environment is going to put great stress on law enforcement. Why? Two reasons. First, all agents will have to become familiar with computers because they are showing up in all different types of cases. A few years back, when you mentioned "computer crime," people said, okay, we are talking high tech hackers, and the FBI has a national computer crime squad so we will put the technically literate agents against the hackers and it will all work out.

Well, the problem is that we do not just see computers in those kinds of hacker cases any more. We kick in the door of drug dealers and find stand-alone PCs with their drug dealing records and their data encrypted or they have hidden files. As we do traditional investigation into fraud, we find we are constantly running into computers, stand-alones, networks, LANs (local area networks), and global area networks. Every agent is constantly running into computers, and that poses problems because, when we deal with computers, we have to be very sensitive to civil liberty issues, which I will address in one second.

The other thing you have to remember about computer crime is that there are no borders. Think about a traditional drug conspiracy case. Someone manufactures narcotics in a foreign country and they want to sell it in the United States. They need people to move it—boats, planes, and cars. When they get it here, they need a distribution network, people. And after it is distributed and they get cash, they need banks. They have to launder the money. All of those things represent opportunities for law enforcement. We catch people at the border bringing in drugs, and we flip them and work them against the organization.

Now think about Markus Hess and the "Cuckoo's Egg." He is sitting in a house in Germany. He dials a local university. He accesses the Internet. He downloads sensitive information. He hangs up the phone. Case closed. Where are the opportunities for law enforcement? Where was the border? Where were the records? You know, in international cases, when we need banking records, banks keep records for a long time. Whether we subpoena them today or tomorrow, they will be there. But in a hacker case like that, once that connection is broken, you cannot trap and trace and find the source. Everything has to be real time, even though it is international, and international cooperation is often not a speedy affair. So it is a real problem for law enforcement.

And another problem is this one. Computers in the national information infrastructure or global information infrastructure clearly show how law enforcement is going to have to adapt to this new technology. Computers have legitimate uses. They are storage devices. But understand they are huge storage devices, and it is getting cheaper and cheaper to store more and more material. What does that mean? It means, when we search in a criminal case, we may get gigabytes of information. Who is going to look at all of that? How are you going to find the needle in that haystack when you are talking about gigabytes?

There are communications devices. They are used as file transfers and electronic mail. There are also publishing devices—newsletters, desktop publishing. From the criminal perspective for law enforcement, computers are targets of offenses. That means that the actor's conduct is designed to steal information from or cause damage to a computer. They are tools of the offense. Computers are used to facilitate traditional offenses. In the old days, if a bank teller wanted to steal money, they would take $10 from the till. Now, you instruct a computer to generate an ATM card, complete with a pin number, without leaving any record that the ATM card was generated. So, they are facilitating traditional offenses. They are incidental to the offense. That is, they are not used directly in the offense, but they are important for law enforcement—like the drug dealer with his records on computer. This is the big problem for the 1990s for law enforcement—or at least a main one. One computer can be used to engage in all those legitimate uses and all those criminal uses at the same time.

So, here is what we have. We have an individual who is importing child pornography from overseas with his computer, and he also has newsletters on AIDS and stamp collecting. And, when we go in and say, "We are seizing your computer because we are taking away the kiddie porn," we are also shutting down the press. This is going to be a constant problem. One of the things we are going to have to look at is innovative ways to solve this problem to make sure that we do not infringe on First Amendment rights, the communications aspect of computers. But, at the same time, we also have to make sure that we enforce the laws that prohibit things such as child porn, copyright infringement, and traditional offenses where computers are used.

James Christy

Mr. Gary: Jim is the director of Computer Crime Investigations for the Air Force Office of Special Investigations (OSI).

   Mr. Christy: What I would like to talk about is how the U.S. Air Force Office of Special Investigations is countering the threat and how we have organized out of necessity.

   This is what the problem really is. We have the Defense Information Systems Agency and the Air Force Information Warfare Center testing our DOD systems to see if they can use the hacker techniques to break into systems. What we are finding is that they are able to gain privilege, get access to those systems, on 88 percent of the systems that they try. That is pretty scary. What is even worse is that only 4 percent of the victims that we test know that they have been victimized. So that is the scope of the problem that we are trying to attack here.

   Some assumptions that we have to make about these kinds of cases are that they are among the most complex cases that OSI gets involved in. They are technical from beginning to end. They are time sensitive. If you do not solve these cases in the first week or so, you are probably not going to find a human body at the other end. They are high visibility, they can do a whole lot of damage quickly, and they are high priority. The impact is instantaneous and disastrous. They commit the crime at the speed of light, and the legal issues are not well framed.

   The uniqueness of a hacker case is that the hacker, the bad guy, never has to be anywhere near the crime scene. Hackers will usually have multiple victims, simultaneously. They will victimize five or six different systems. They could be distributed anywhere in the world and it all happens at the same time.

   The air force is rarely the sole target. I do not run a case where it is just going to be air force systems that have been attacked. I am going to have civilian systems, army systems, and academic systems. Usually we involve multiple investigative jurisdictions. Typically, law enforcement jurisdiction is geographical. These things transcend geographical boundaries. Virtually all of my cases start out as unknown subject cases. I have absolutely no idea who is doing this to us or where they are.

   So, here is my pool of subjects when we start. We have our Internet users, about 15 million, and anybody with a computer, a modem, and access to the phone lines worldwide. Everybody here has been talking a little bit about the Internet. We have 92 countries currently connected to the Internet, and that is probably growing on a daily basis. There are 7.5 million users here in the United States, 15 million users worldwide. That is as of March, so I have no idea what the figures are now. [Recent reports indicate that the number of Internet users has reached 20 million and that Internet is now accessible to more than 130 nations.] Somebody was telling me that, at this current growth rate, growth would come to a complete halt at the year 2001, and that is because everybody in the world would then have Internet access.

What I would like to talk about is a particular case that we are just finishing up now at Rome Air Development Center at Griffith's Air Force Base in New York. This is a typical case. Rome, up in New York, was attacked. We went in. They noticed that they had a hacker intrusion. We sent our Information Warfare Center, our computer security people from the air force along with a team of my computer crime investigators up there. What they found was that 30 systems at Rome Air Development Center had been compromised. We were talking earlier about sniffers. We found six sniffers on those 30 systems that were gathering user IDs and passwords for other systems.

We were attacked from two major locations, but we were actually attacked during this time frame from about 10 different locations. The two main sites were commercial sites, one in New York and one in Seattle. And over this 26-day period, we had more than 150 intrusions by two hackers.

We were not the only victim. We went to our sources. We set up a technical surveillance to gather evidence at Rome. It was almost like going in with night vision glasses—for a change. Usually, when we set up monitoring, the hackers can see us, and it is like roaches heading for the walls when you turn the lights on. This time, we went in with night vision glasses, and we just watched the hacker activity while we were trying to trace them back. The individual was using the Internet, but he was also making fraudulent use of the phone system. Hence, the technology was not there for us to trace the hacker back. So, we went to our informants' network. We said, "We are getting hit by two individuals, someone using the name Data Stream and the other using the name Kuji. Somebody please tell us where these people are and who they are?" A source came forward and said, "Yes, I had a conversation. Here is an E-mail that I had with the individual back in January. He said that he liked to attack DOT-MIL sites because they were so insecure. He lives in the UK, and here is his phone number because he has a bulletin board there, an electronic bulletin board."

We called Scotland Yard. Scotland Yard immediately set up monitoring on the individual, and within two hours we had a correlation. Every time we had an intrusion at Rome, the individual was on-line, using fraudulent phone methods, "freaking," to get out of the UK. And where was he going? From the time that he logged on in the UK until he ended up at Rome usually took him 30 minutes. What he was doing is called "looping" and "weaving." He was using multiple sites and multiple countries as a conduit to help prevent us from tracing him back. He was going through multiple countries in South America, multiple countries in Europe, and through Mexico to end up at Rome.

Once he got through all the systems at Rome, we watched where he went. We had more than 100 victims that were downstream from Rome. Some of the major victims were NASA, the jet propulsion laboratory in California, and the Goddard Space Flight Center here in Greenbelt, Maryland. We actually had Scotland Yard circling his house, getting ready to arrest him with one of my computer crime investigators alongside. And we said, "Okay, the plan is, as soon as he's on-line at Rome, we will let him stay on-line for about 10 to 15 minutes then you guys go break the door down."

Well, all of a sudden, we got him on-line. We communicated with Scotland Yard. They are circling the house, and all of a sudden he goes to South Korea and does what is called a "world mount." He picked up all the disk space from the South Korean Atomic Research Institute and moved it to Rome. So we stopped the operation at that point and decided to monitor a little bit longer. Scotland Yard then waited about two weeks before they executed their search warrant and arrested the 16-year-old. Scotland Yard said that, when they actually pulled him away from the keyboard up on the third floor and he realized what had happened, he curled up in a fetal position on the floor and cried.

We have another hacker, Kuji. We have no idea who he is or where he came from. He was far more sophisticated than Data Stream. He never stayed on-line very long. And everything that Data Stream got, Kuji got, but we still have no idea who Kuji is.

So, the upshot of this intrusion was that although we had only two hackers, we had 26 days of attacks, and 20 days of monitoring. We found six different sniffers on the Rome systems alone. There were also 150 intrusions during that time frame from 10 different points of origin and at least eight different countries used as conduits. This is just a list of the victims that we know about. We do not know all the victims between the UK and Rome Air Development Center; but these are the downstream victims.

What we have done to counter this threat within OSI is to centrally manage these cases. My office runs all the hacker intrusion cases for the air force because we have so many victims simultaneously around the world we could have five or six different OSI offices running simultaneous, parallel cases. We do not have those kinds of resources, and we need to be able to correlate the events that are occurring. If we have each individual geographic area running its own case on their victim and not coordinating the effort, we are wasting a lot of our time and we are not going to be really successful. So, it is kind of one-stop shopping for the air force for intrusion cases.

All of our computer crime investigators have a minimum of five years' experience in the computer field before they come on board, and we train them as investigators. Lots of law enforcement agencies go out and hire attorneys and accountants. We go out and hire computer specialists because we need their technical background in these kinds of cases from beginning to end.

And then we have to liaise with all the other law enforcement agencies. We work regularly with Scott Charney in the Secret Service and the FBI. We have to. We go to international conferences where we deal with Scotland Yard and the Australian Federal Police, because they are all in the loop and we have to coordinate the efforts. We also work with Dain's group, CERT, and all the other CERTs around the world, because they are going to know the person to contact in their country and the right person in law enforcement that we need to talk to coordinate these efforts because this is a global problem.

As for technical surveillances, we are still in the process of developing techniques to allow us to detect, first of all, that we have an intrusion ongoing and then to be able to collect that evidence and then go through it so that we can give the boiled-down version to the prosecutor for our search warrants and for the prosecution. Even then, technical surveillance and technology are not going to solve these cases for us. We still need the human informants out there that are going to come forward and tell us who the Data Streams of the world are. We also attend hacker conferences to get to know the enemy.

One of the key points is centralization. These kinds of cases have to be centrally managed—cases are managed out of our office. They have to be that way. Another key point is education—education for the users as well as education for law enforcement. We all have senior managers. The senior managers have to admit that there is a problem and put resources toward it. Then we probably need legislation to help us.

Question and Answer Session

Question: Let me kick it off while you are collecting your thoughts. I do not know who could answer this, but could a man—who is not prone to curling up in the fetal position such as Saddam Hussein—using supercomputers and super hackers, have paralyzed vital nerve centers in this country before Desert Shield became Desert Storm?

Mr. Christy: Yes, absolutely. The analogy that was made to me was that we are the biggest, baddest person in the bar, but we have a glass jaw. So, yes, we are just as vulnerable as everybody else.

Mr. Gary: I should also add that in the Legion of Doom case in Atlanta, in debriefing the hackers after they had been prosecuted, they told us that they had the ability to shut down phone systems throughout the entire southeastern United States because they totally controlled Bell South's computers.

Mr. Parker: We found at least 25 malicious hackers in Europe and in the United States who claimed, and convinced us, that they could shut down major sections of the

U.S. telephone system through strictly software kinds of attacks, not blowing up switches or anything. They also indicated, however, that it would require insiders in the telephone systems themselves to accomplish this.

And we also found this new generation of hackers are starting to use high paid informants within the criminal justice agencies and within the telephone companies. They are making large amounts of money through software piracy, game piracy, and reselling telephone services in order to pay their informants who are also young hackers, but who are engaged in full-time employment in telephone systems.

Mr. Christy: During Desert Shield, two days before Iraq invaded Kuwait, we had a young hacker who had broken into a system at the Pentagon from the local area. He pleaded guilty. So, between that time and the time when he was sentenced, we asked him to help us out. I sat him down in an office over at Bolling Air Force Base and had him go in and attack as many air force systems as he could get into.

The plan was that we have centralized management of computer security, down at Kelly Air Force Base in San Antonio. We wired this kid up so that everything that he did was recorded. We put a video camera on him and told him to go hack air force systems. We would identify the vulnerability and then wait for the victim to come back to the security office and tell them that they had been victimized. Then the security office would go out and tell them how to fix the problem. We would not tell them that it was OSI that did it to them.

So, we sat him down, and, within 15 seconds he broke into the same computer at the Pentagon that he was convicted for because they still had not fixed the vulnerabilities. I had to go back the next day and tell the emperor he still had no clothes. We did this operation for about three weeks. During that three-week time frame, he broke into over 200 air force systems. Zero victims reported that they had been hacked into. Not one. Now we are getting ready to go to war, and nobody is monitoring the system because they do not have the tools available, or the education or experience.

Mr. Gary: This technology, these techniques are available. If organized crime needs someone to pilot an aircraft, they will hire someone to do that. If they need any particular special skill, they can hire someone to do that. That is exactly what we see happening. The 16-year-old that went into the fetal position once apprehended in England was the one that was apprehended. Jim was talking about the other individual; they still do not have a clue as to who that was.

When I mentioned that Internet is a laboratory, I am absolutely sincere when I say that to you. We are seeing, unfortunately, the ones that are learning how to do this from the more practiced, the more experienced. Often, new techniques are introduced with inexperienced people to see what results you will get. That affords the real expert, the real brain, some cushion, some buffering, if you would.

Richard Helms: As an individual who was totally unwashed and untutored in the computer world, what I do not quite understand is how one goes through these networks all over the world at no charge. If you want to make a telephone call to London, it costs you some money. You apparently have an arrangement in the computer world where everything is free. Why is it not high time that you put a charge on some of this?

Mr. Gary: No, these are different philosophies; it is the connection that you pay for in a monthly rate or an annual rate whatever you use that connection for. For the actual packet, the actual information transversing the network, there is not a per-unit charge like there would be in the telephone system.

Mr. Helms: How does a 16-year-old hacker have enough money to keep doing this day after day after day?

Mr. Gary: A company has a large PBX system to handle all their telephone calls. They have a service for their employees who are traveling so that they can call an 800 number, go into the PBX of that company, and, using a two-digit code like 25, then be switched to an outgoing long distance telephone number for which the company pays the bill.

We have young people in Germany who are selling these services to Turkish guest workers. The Turkish guest worker is set up on one of these 800 calls that comes into a large company in the United States and is given the two-digit code, which allows him to then dial another number in Turkey. The hackers are using this same technique.

I got a call at 9:00 last Thursday night. I answered the call and there were 49 hackers on the line because that is the maximum number you can get on an international conference call. Some of them spoke with accents, obviously from other parts of the world. They conversed with me in a meeting for about an hour, asking me why I say all these bad things about them. None of them, of course, were paying for any of that telephone service.

Mr. Christy: We have seen many, many cases now where hackers make local calls to universities in their own area, like in the "Cuckoo's Egg." You call a university in your own area that may have a fairly open system. Once you log on and you are in that university, when you start sending transmissions to other universities or to Rome, you look like an authorized user of that first university. Your call is only a local call, so you are not running up any charges.

Judge William Sessions: About 10 days ago, I saw an article about the publishing of an encryption code on, I think, Internet from one company's encryption code. Can you discuss that type of thing and the dangers that you see?

Mr. Parker: One of the single most powerful controls we have over information is the use of cryptography. That is the scrambling of information, using a secret key at one site, and then decrypting, using another secret key at another site. The communication using this powerful crypto capability is becoming a serious threat, because all of the security of the information that is encrypted is now focused in the secrecy of these keys.

The crypto is so strong that it cannot be decrypted using brute force methods. The administration of the keys, however, now becomes critical. And capturing a 128-character key becomes a critical activity. If it is sent in clear text across the line, obviously, it is going to be picked up, because there are thousands of kids monitoring all these communications, looking for those keys.

Question: I would like to ask the panel about how the legal system is handling this? If the hacker is based in a country without extradition, without an MLAT [Multilateral Assistance Treaty], what can you do? How can you prosecute a case that could be this complicated, that takes all kinds of technical expertise to understand, with a jury of, say, 12 people who fell off the subway? What incentives are there for law enforcement people to get on stuff that is this complicated when they are knee-deep in cases that are, let us say, videotaped drug transactions in high quality color?

Mr. Charney: On the international front, there has been a move afoot for some time to coordinate international efforts against computer crime. Both the Organization of Economic Cooperation and Development in Paris, which recently issued the guidelines for the security of information systems, and the Council of Europe have been working on projects designed to harmonize computer crime laws and also eliminate some of the procedural hurdles that are involved in computer crime investigations.

We still have a long way to go, but what has happened is, as the problem has increased, most countries like the United States have recognized that they need dedicated computer crime units. So, New Scotland Yard, the Australian Federal Police, and the RCMP are all developing that level of expertise and have been working closely with U.S. law enforcement to make sure we can get virtually instantaneous assistance in these kinds of cases. We recently had a case where the attack was on the Department of Commerce at NOAA. Within 60 days, we had arrests in Denmark.

As for the jury issue, when Robert Morris launched the Morris Worm in 1988 that shut down about 6,000 computers around the world, his case went to trial, and, in fact, none of the jurors even had a college education. It is really an issue of getting the proper witnesses to explain this technology. One of the problems has always been that when you are working computer crime cases, there is a lingo. There is a dictionary all its own.

In hiring attorneys to work in my unit, I have always taken the position that I can teach a good lawyer the technology, but I cannot teach a technocrat how to become a good lawyer. This stuff, in all fairness, is hard, but it is not that hard. What we did, for example, in the Morris Worm case was call people from academia, who testified and explained how the Internet works, what a worm is, and why this is a problem. We were successful in that case, and we will continue to do that.

Mr. Gary: But your observation is absolutely valid. In this country, we have 48 to 50 different interpretations of what computer crime is and what constitutes evidence with regard to a particular crime. Internationally, it is just compounded. In some countries, they have recently changed the laws because there was no computer crime specified or defined, it was not an issue.

There is an interesting point I want to make. The Robert Morris worm infected 6,000 sites in the United States; this was just one incident. We had a single incident a year-and-a-half ago, a single incident that involved 65,000 computer sites. That happened to be one that originated in Australia. It used a compromised system in New England to attack 65,000 computers in Europe over one weekend.

That is the magnitude of the problem. That is how quickly things move, and your point is exactly right. It is and has been a tremendous problem. But the community has recognized that—a small portion of the community—and is working. We cooperate very, very well with the agencies that Scott had mentioned. The Dutch Federal Police are involved. So there is a foundation beginning to develop in this arena, but it is a technical one. We still are not at the policy level. We are still not there.

Question: Mr. Parker, with respect to the absolute privacy issue, how do you deal with the strong cryptography that is available abroad, say in Russia?

Mr. Parker: The problem, obviously, has to be addressed on an international basis, and there are complaints that U.S. laws and regulations are very strict in the export of cryptographic capabilities. But there are other countries where it is also even more restricted, and there are other countries, obviously, where there are no restrictions at all.

Whatever is done, we are dealing with the low-watermark level of our vulnerabilities. Until we have fixed the greatest vulnerability, then everything is measured on that greatest vulnerability. So, any kind of control of crypto has got to be done through international agreements.

Now, we have international agreements for maritime. There are all kinds of international agreements and laws concerning maritime. I do not see any reason why we cannot extend this concept and agree on the equivalent of maritime laws for the control of cryptographic protection of information. But it requires a tremendous amount of dedication on the part of a large number of very high-level people to accomplish it, and I suspect we will have to have some major cryptographic disasters before there is enough attention to treat it at that level.

Mr. Gary: We are talking about technology, we are talking about information available in the networks. If you consider the national health programs, for example, and your own health records and information about yourself, your family, and your spouse being available to the international community through these computer networks, you begin to appreciate some of the significance of the exposure here. The fact is that some protection mechanisms do exist, but we are not seeing those techniques, those technologies, being incorporated until after the fact.

If you would like to wait that long, it will probably happen. But one of the things that we are doing at CERT is the reactive portion of this activity: responding to a site that has been compromised, that has been intruded, and trying to help them determine what happened and how to correct it. That is certainly necessary, but it is certainly not sufficient. We have got to get more proactive in this and teach people and make them at least understand the vulnerabilities that exist in network information systems.

We used to talk about insider threat and outsider threat. Probably everyone has heard that terminology and that reference. In the network world, nearly everyone is inside. Every time you connect your computer to another system, you have just incorporated a whole other community of users as insiders. The law firm that has a major client that wants to connect the systems together because it will facilitate communications and so forth now has to be concerned about what system it is. What other systems is that client connected to? What other hospital or pharmaceutical organization?

We do not normally think about these issues until after the fact. One of our missions at CERT and the community that we represent is to try to raise the awareness and level of understanding and appreciation so that people at least will be cognizant of these issues, of these vulnerabilities, and take some appropriate basic steps to improve the situation.

In this world of right-sizing and down-sizing organizations, we have basically organized out the real technicians, the really capable individuals, and they have left, sometimes as very disgruntled employees. If you think about this, this is less than ideal. These are people who know your system better than the ones who remain, and they are not at all happy about the situation. If we talk about an opportunity for someone to buy information or buy techniques to compromise your system—whether you are a state government, the Social Security Administration, the air force, or whether you are J.P. Morgan—the technologies, again, directly relate to all these environments.

Question: It seems that some of the antagonists have more celebrity status than punitive. Are there any indications about some common benchmarking with regard to the sentencing of those involved in this?

Mr. Charney: There are two things to note. First of all, the sentences seem to be increasing. Hackers are now going to jail with some regularity, which is a change from where we were before. Second, the U.S. Sentencing Commission is looking at a Justice Department proposal to change the way computer criminals are sentenced by considering other factors in determining what the appropriate sentence should be.

Right now, under the current sentencing scheme, the major issue is the amount of financial damaged caused to the victim. In many of these cases, it is very hard to find a dollar loss if you are talking about information and the cost of system recovery and even checking your system. For example, we had a recent case where a hacker went through Boeing on his way to the U.S. District Court in Seattle where his scheme was, apparently, to commute his own sentence. Although he did not alter the Boeing systems, it still cost them around $75,000 to check all the data in their computers because they could not run the risk that something had been altered. And, in a lot of the cases where people are accessing credit reporting information, the concern is not just the dollar amount—a credit report may be worth only $1 for a commercial customer—but, rather, the significant invasion of privacy that occurs.

Working with the Sentencing Commission's Computer Crime Working Group, we have agreed in principle on some commentary language where judges will start looking beyond merely dollar loss and look at things like substantial invasion of privacy. We hope to be able to move on that as soon as the Sentencing Commission gets full staffing.

Question: Have you seen any increase in computer hacking or computer crimes generated out of the former Soviet Union or Eastern bloc? I saw on some of the slides references to Latvia and other countries. Do we see anything unusual about that?

Mr. Christy: We are seeing a lot more coming out of the European side of the house. In this particular case, it was due to the old analog phone system that he had and the freaking technique that this individual was using. We are seeing it come from basically everywhere. I mean, nobody is an island anymore.

Mr. Parker: There are lots of angry programmers in Russia and Bulgaria, in particular, as we have seen from an increase of very virulent computer viruses. I think connectivity is the key to it. As these countries gain in their connectivity to the rest of the world through telephone communications, we will probably see a significant increase in problems that emanate from those areas. They have nothing to lose.

Mr. Charney: Exactly right. Statistically, you are correct, and Donn, I think, has provided the key you have to keep in mind. As they move further into the technologies, they have more access. And as they have more access, as more people come into the system, you are going to find that a certain percentage of them will have other than desirable objectives. There are cases, documented cases, in the PC virus world. For example, they have an academy in Bulgaria that teaches about and perfects computer viruses. The Internet right now is 3,100,000 computers linked together internationally. You may not be familiar with that system and that spine, but there are certain domains. The DOT MIL is the military domain. The DOT GOV is the government domain, and the DOT COM, is the commercial world. That is how you identify each other electronically.

So, in the Internet, we are growing at a tremendous rate. But the largest domain of growth is the DOT COM. There are more commercial users coming into the Internet. They are coming by the trainload, and the largest geographic area of growth is offshore. We are finding that the Internet is growing exponentially overseas, and that, coupled with the large number of new commercial users, causes us grave concern.

I very much respect the attitude that in business you accept a certain amount of risk. Our concern is that the business users do not completely understand the risk. They do not appreciate the full magnitude of the risks they are taking as they enter this network. If they did, I would say the decision is sound, but I am a little pessimistic.

CHAPTER 4

Maintaining the Security, Integrity, and Efficiency of our Financial System in a Global Criminal Market

Stanley E. Morris
Director, Financial Crimes Enforcement Network
(FinCEN)

Judge Webster: Stanley Morris and I first became acquainted when he came with the Reagan administration into the Justice Department as a deputy to the deputy attorney general. He was the first non-lawyer that I had run into in the Justice Department, and one that I watched at first with some skepticism as to what was he doing there, only to realize that Stan was an extraordinarily gifted person, particularly in the area of policy formulation. In all the conferences I attended, both on-site and off-site, Stan was one of the leaders. He enjoyed the confidence of William French Smith and was an exceptional contributor in the area of crime solving problems.

He was good enough to be asked to become the director of the marshal service, where he served from 1983 to 1989. Among many responsibilities, he had charge of the very difficult Witness Protection Program, which, as you know, protects the witnesses who are willing to make the difficult choice of testifying for the government, then trying to live in anonymity and not be assassinated. We have only to think of the tragedy with Magistrate Falcone just a year or so ago in Italy to appreciate the high price that people pay for cooperating with their governments in an effort to deal with dangerous organized crime.

From 1989 to 1991, Stan was deputy director for supply reduction in the White House Office of National Drug Control Policy (the drug czar), where he directed the U.S. domestic and international drug control strategies. During his tenure, as in many other assignments he has had, he worked closely with government and law enforcement entities inside and outside the United States to carry on competent and effective anti-drug activities.

He currently is director of the Financial Crimes Enforcement Network—FinCEN. One of the few acronyms I can pronounce. FinCEN had gone through some significant reorganizations at the time that Stan was asked to take over as director, in May of this year. Simultaneously, the responsibility for the Office of Financial Enforcement, which is a separate Treasury organization, was transferred to FinCEN, thus making Stan Morris the first director to head the newly created alliance between FinCEN and the Office of Financial Enforcement, which dealt with money laundering and related crimes.

It is a tremendously important responsibility at a tremendously important time. Those of us who know Stan know that he is equal to the challenge. He, incidentally, was part of the group that went with Louis Freeh to Russia. He has just finished another interesting conference that I hope he is going to talk to us about today.

Stanley Morris

It is truly significant that an audience as distinguished and varied as this one is focusing on the emergence of a global criminal market at the invitation of a policy organization with a very distinguished record. It will require groups with the backgrounds, experiences, and insights of this audience to pool our talents if we are to appreciate the threat of organized crime and what to do about it.

Maintenance of the security, integrity, and efficiency of our financial system is at the heart of the mission of the Department of Treasury and its enforcement activities. Tax and trade fraud, money laundering, narcotic smuggling, sophisticated counterfeiting, penetration of computer and electronic communication systems, trafficking, and weapons all strike directly at the sanctity of the international financial system. They are all characteristic of what you are discussing today and of what we are very worried about.

I would like to be clear from the outset. First, whether we are bankers, communication specialists, corporate executives, regulators, intelligence analysts, or law enforcement officers, we must come to grips firmly and effectively with increasingly elusive, well-financed, and technologically adept criminal enterprises. Those enterprises are determined to use every means available to subvert the financial systems that are the very cornerstone of international commerce.

Second, our challenge does not come simply from a new government mandate or the search for a new security mission. As the corporate officials and private security experts here today can tell you, it is a question of conduct that costs businesses billions of dollars a year and increasingly undermines the assumption on which free market commerce must be based.

Third, the complexity of the threat we face requires a sophisticated and, in some ways, an iconoclastic response. To be blunt, you have got to be prepared to break some bureaucratic eggs and tear down some pretty old walls if we want to get anything meaningful done.

Nothing is new, of course, about profit and greed as a motive for crime, or about organized criminal gangs working across national borders. Take this intelligence report. On the morning of June 26th, a cashier and a bank clerk drove through St. Petersburg with two policemen and five soldiers. They were carrying millions of dollars of rubles in an interbank transfer. But 10 persons were waiting to rob the vehicle in Erivan Square, acting on information from corrupt government officials that the bank transfer was about to occur.

The leader of the robbers was dressed as an army officer and created turmoil in the square by warning people that violence was expected. When the bankers and their escort arrived, they were intercepted by the conspirators using explosives and weapons, and the currency was stolen. The stolen currency was hidden in a government building in the Caucasus Mountains until it was smuggled across the border into Germany a month after the robbery.

Then, five months later, the gang sought to launder the currency by placing it in small amounts, smurfing it in banks across Northern Europe on a single day. At that point, the launderers and at least some of the ring leaders were arrested on information supplied by a German undercover officer to German police and shared with Russian police. There, you have all the elements of the problem: violent robbery, corruption, smuggling of currency, money laundering. And, interestingly, the same gang had stolen currency plates and was experimenting with making counterfeit rubles.

In fact, the events I described did take place in June, but in June of 1907. They were part of what has been called the most famous of all revolutionary robberies. It was staged by the Bolsheviks before 1917. That organized crime activity ultimately succeeded in toppling a nation. The fact that the anecdote sounds as current as this morning's *Financial Times* raises a question. Why special attention to organized crime today and why now? I would give you three quick answers: the international dimensions of the problem, the resources and technology at the command of the criminals, and the risk their conduct poses at this point in the development of the world financial trading systems.

You have heard today, and will hear later, the details of various aspects of international crime. Without trying to take away from those presentations, let me cite a few observations that we have made at FinCEN. First, the profits of crime that are bled into the financial system each year are staggering, detrimental by any calculation. The debates about the amount of money laundered annually are continuing, and it may well be impossible to pinpoint the amount. One year's figure is at $30 billion, $55 billion, or $100 billion simply as a result of U.S. drug sales. Total laundered funds worldwide could easily amount to close to $300 billion because it is crystal clear to any of us who have looked at this issue that it is more than narcotic profits alone. It is tax and tariff evasion, arms smuggling, terrorism, and a raft of financial frauds.

At the Financial Action Task Force Meeting two weeks ago, I sat next to a representative from Finland. I learned from the Finnish representative that 50 percent, half, of all the suspicious transaction activities being reported by Finnish institutions involve deposits by Russians. Needless to say, the Finns are very nervous.

The skills of our counterfeiters are ever expanding. Trade and tax fraud cost governments hundreds of billions of dollars each year around the world and have made predictable fiscal policies for developing economies increasingly difficult, if not impossible, to shape.

Last week, we at FinCEN cohosted a five-day conference to share information about Russian organized crime groups operating in central and western Europe and in the United States. The conference was attended by close to 400 law enforcement and intelligence analysts, 50 from overseas. When I considered the presentations ranging across the spectrum of criminal conduct, I, at least for one, made a stark conclusion. The levels of violence and corruption being effectively exported from Russia today as it struggles to establish free institutions are likely as great, if perhaps not even far greater, than at any time during Soviet rule.

As troubling as these facts are, they are not the most important part of the story. More important are the character of the groups we face and the particularly propitious time at which they find themselves operating. When we say that organized crime is a multinational enterprise, we are saying more than the heroin grown in the Golden Triangle ends up being sold in Boston for cash laundered through Houston, or that computer criminals in London can steal funds electronically from banks in Perth. Organized crime has become, in the last 10 or so years, a bastion of highly developed—if sadly misdirected—business and management skills. Its managers view crime as a true investment in export commodity from their seats, whether they be in Palermo, Moscow, Hong Kong, Lagos, Kingston, or New York.

The groups about which we know the most are operated by people who want to make money and are accustomed to, indeed, even thrive on what we would recognize as market discipline. They know how to trade, how to seek and take advantage of opportunities, and how to manage integrated enterprises. There is every indication that they are increasingly interested in moving back and forth between legal and illegal activity and are finding the line between the two increasingly easy to cross. That is why crimes such as money laundering have taken on such importance to Treasury staffs and enforcement professionals around the world.

The money laundering experience also teaches us something else. Although these groups are increasingly involved in legitimate activity, they devote much creativity to attempting to structure their affairs to thwart detection. That leads to the second factor, the opportunities offered to such groups by the world situation—both at the macro and at the micro level.

We have worked for decades to foster the movement to free democratic institutions and to increasingly open trade around the world. Those have been standards upon which U.S. foreign policy was framed. But the changing world order creates vast wedges for crooks. As markets open up, organized criminals can move in. The cash available to the Russian mob organizations, for example, gives them an extraordinary opportunity to dominate fledgling sectors of the legitimate economy as few legitimate firms or business people are able to do.

On the micro level, we see the ability of any individual using a relatively inexpensive computer and a common telephone line to move enormous masses of data around the world at nearly the speed of light. Messages of many sorts can then become easier to send and to encrypt, and money can be moved instantly, whether to finance building a hospital or purchase stolen weapons or nuclear materials. So, when we combine the individual empowerment that technology brings with the openings created by the fall of the Soviet system and resulting social changes covering close to half the globe, it is obvious that the opportunities for criminal success, especially focused, well-trained criminals, increases exponentially and so does the risk that their conduct can cause.

First, criminal activities, if unchecked, will be, indeed is, increasingly destabilizing for political and economic reform. This is certainly true of Russia, but the problem is by no means limited to reconstruction of societies in the newly independent states. As history has time and time again shown us, political stability, democracy, and free markets depend on solvent, stable, and honest financial, commercial, and trading systems. If the Italian Mafia were a nation, its narcotics proceeds alone would likely make it the twentieth richest nation in the world, richer than 150 sovereign states. If it has reached the economic and political power it holds from its base in Italy, consider the potential from tightly organized groups operating on the far bigger stage created by the independence of the states of the former Soviet Union or by the massive economic changes sweeping China and East Asia.

Our current concerns are not just about violence or drugs or even criminal takeovers of certain industries. It is about a more general loss of faith. What ultimately is involved is the legitimacy of our trading and financial systems and the commitment to the rules by ordinary citizens, without which civil society cannot be sustained. There is a wry comment that "Russia is still a Marxist country. Having endured Marx's vision of socialism, it is now enduring Marx's vision of anarchic capitalism." That may be an intellectual's jive, but I wonder if a lot of eastern European citizens do not say the same thing, perhaps in somewhat earthier language.

White collar crime often seems transparent because its direct effect on any particular citizen is relatively small. The victims are defused. A billion dollar theft of assets spread over the population of a large country does not amount to much, perhaps, but the cumulative effect of such conduct and the power that it gives to those who conduct it is clearly debilitating. Tax collection, for example, must depend to a large degree on voluntary compliance. A nation that cannot reasonably expect a certain level of commercial activity to generate a certain level of government revenue simply cannot hope to deal with its budget needs or to strengthen its currency. At least some observers have attributed Poland's economic difficulties several years ago not to mistakes and projections of its planners about growth rates but to their failure to understand that receiving tax revenues is not simply a matter of multiplying a level of output by some marginal rate. Taxes do not just pour in. A payment system has to be created, administered, enforced, and, finally and most important, accepted by the citizenry.

An equal risk is the fate of the enormous sums of aid that the United States and its political and financial partners have devoted to assisting development. Organized crime and the corruption it inevitably brings whittle down those funds incountry. It hampers the health and competitive ability of honest enterprises and puts a brake on international investment.

I heard a story from a development professional working on an international project, and it is worth repeating for what it portends. The project involved financing a new factory. The uses of the monies raised by the financing included not only the normal costs for planning, construction, operation, and salaries, but also salaries for a protection detail, designed to secure the factory to be built from thugs working for various gangs in the country involved. That is a frightening specter, as *60 Minutes* reported recently. We cannot expect international investment to grow if such investment means carrying on business either in competition with or by paying protection fees to criminal syndicates. Yet, in many of the countries around the world, that is precisely what is going on.

We recognize that there is an international criminal economy that mirrors and that often abuses the international economy generally. Treasury is committed to an international strategy for dealing with financial crime, not just as a matter of policy but as a clear matter of necessity. This is a crucial point.

The final communiqué of this year's G-7 meeting in Naples (attended by President Clinton, Secretary Bentsen, and the leaders and finance ministers of the United Kingdom, France, Germany, Italy, Canada, and Japan) states plainly that "organized trends in national crime, including money laundering, and the use of illicit proceeds to take control of legitimate business is a worldwide problem." Well, if that is the case, then what sorts of programs can we develop to deal with the problem?

Treasury Under Secretary Ronald Noble testified last week that an effective anti-money laundering strategy has to combine prevention, detection, and enforcement. I think the same is true of our deployment of resources against organized commercial crime across the board and around the world. I would like to be, perhaps, a little more blunt today. If we really care to make a difference, we have got to stop doing business according to narrow parochial distinctions and traditions that our criminal adversaries are only too happy to exploit all the way, as they like to say, to the bank.

We should be tired of trying to cope in a professional world that separates enforcement and regulation or public and private sectors, a world where agencies do not talk to one another—and this is true of intelligence agencies as well as law enforcement agencies. It is even true within parts of the same agencies. The first step is to stop pretending that we operate in our own worlds like some hedgehogs trying to outwit the foxes. Because if we do, we will fail.

Two weeks ago, I spoke at a meeting in Germany. It is ironic that it was one of the first times that bankers, investigators, and regulators had ever been brought together to talk about this problem. But it is bankers, not policemen, that see the money launderers first. And it is businessmen, not police or intelligence officers, who see the gangs up close. To try to get a handle on the problem, while somehow separating what private sector and public sector officials do, is not going to work, not for a minute.

Second, we have to throw away our mission-based myopia. There is a natural tendency that we all share to continue doing our old jobs in the face of new problems. Every enforcement agency that I have been involved with tends to define the problem based upon the tools it has. If it has a hammer, then it concludes the problem must be a nail. If it has historically used a wrench, it concludes the problem must be a bolt. We have got to get beyond this sort of parochial thinking if we are to undertake a successful attack on the issue as complex as organized crime in the world today.

Building new tools, though, requires an even broader change. Our attempts to deal with organized crime run counter to the way performance and success have traditionally been measured in law enforcement. In law enforcement, we are evaluated on arrests, seizures, prosecutions. These are all important, but they are not and do not measure prevention. The advocates of community policing in our neighborhoods ask listeners to compare the following statistics: 100 arrests made in the 8th District, or 5 arrests made in the 8th District. The first sounds better unless the second reflects the fact not of less efficiency but of the need for fewer arrests because the fact of reduced levels of crime. But no one has yet built the architecture to measure prevention performance. That is why conferences like this are so important. Conceptual changes of the sort necessary do not and probably cannot happen overnight, but we must begin.

We are also used to dividing enforcement jurisdictionally and in distinguishing enforcement from regulation and the public sector from the private sector. But, now, we cannot ignore the playing fields of the whole economy in which our adversaries operate. Take money laundering. We worked for 10 years to upgrade compliance at the nation's banks and we have come a long way. So, what has happened? The launderers have moved to nonbank institutions (check cashers, money order sellers, companies that specialize in changing currency or sending funds abroad) that are not on the financial regulators' radar screen.

No, but they are on the cartels' radar screens. The cartels over- or understate invoices or simply buy goods for export and resell them to raise cash abroad. That is what we mean. The issue is not how to clean up banks or brokers or casas de cambios, it is how to make a dent in money laundering or trade fraud or computer fraud. This is significantly more difficult to measure.

This does not suggest a public sector takeover or more regulation or anything of the sort. We have to recognize and build upon a partnership between the public and private sector and between nations to standardize our approaches, share intelligence, and limit the harm that this sort of crime can do to our economies and to our citizens. So, let us face it, as long as these groups can find havens, they will, indeed, move.

In some ways, what I am proposing sounds perhaps a bit like expanded community policing, something we might call financial community policing. If by that we mean that simple enforcement after the fact can never hope to do the job, what can we do specifically and immediately?

First, we have got to tackle compartmentalization in our own backyards. At Treasury, we are trying to put into place new regulations that place increased responsibilities on banks, but at the same time treat our banks not as mechanical reporters but as partners in solving a problem that affects them as much as it does us. We want them to put in place money laundering policies and procedures—many already have, including some whose representatives are here today—and help us figure out where the money will go when we push the problem where. We are also imposing the same responsibilities on other financial intermediaries.

Second, we have got to get used to real cooperation, not lip-service attempts that get killed in endless interagency working groups. We all know the differences when we want to know them. We are beginning to engage in a wide-ranging program at Treasury for nonparochial electronic sharing of information. For example, we are placing state enforcement agencies on-line to various currency movement reports within Treasury. We have seen an astounding rate of usefulness in the information already. We have also moved to try to share information among agencies and are hoping to find ways to provide far more information than we have in the past back to the financial community. But we are not successful in how to measure what it is we are doing because we are not directly involved in the arrest, prosecution, seizures, and the like. Yet, it is precisely that activity, it seems to me, that is so essential in dealing with a complex issue like organized crime.

Third, technical assistance is essential. Budgets are tight, but it is in our own interest to work wherever we can in cooperation with other nations to upgrade the training and potential of their police, tax, customs administrators, banking, and commercial systems.

Fourth, we need to exert all of our influence, knowledge, and experience in raising standards around the globe. As you discussed this morning, some countries are at present simply more susceptible than others to the inroads of organized crime. One of the basic thrusts of the Financial Action Task Force is that all nations must deal with the implications of international money laundering before the international effort can be successful. It is a weak link issue, and we need to strengthen all links.

That is a point about which there should be no confusion. We are guilty of parochialism, nationally and internationally. Law enforcement seems, too often, to bring out the worst in all of us. Anyone who has attended police conferences around the world, as many people in this room know all too well, find that the same stories are repeated over and over . . . state and local police who do not talk to federal police or vice versa. There is competition between domestic police and customs officials, between diplomats and police attachÇs and the intelligence analysts.

I think, finally, that the problems we are grappling with today should remind us all of something quite basic. Enforcement is government's quality control function. Enforcement is often a bit of a stepchild in government circles, an after-the-fact activity designed to make sure rule-breakers are punished as the law allows. But in the situation we find ourselves in today, as millions seek to develop thoroughly new civil societies on much of the European land mass, as trading barriers fall, and as communications shrink our world, it is simply impossible not to ask about enforcement as plans are made and decisions taken. Our enforcement people can answer questions that our civil people never even know are questions.

Free societies operate on the basis of rules and limits, on whose observance a great deal depends. Rules that cannot be enforced or administered do more harm than good. So, the issues we are facing and that you are discussing today remind us that enforcement is not simply a matter of individual prosecutions or investigations. It is government's quality control function and is at the core of the implementation of policy. It must be viewed as the continuation of the policy. That sentence, of course, is a paraphrase of Clausewitz.

I am not suggesting that organized crime should be viewed as a sort of strategic threat to world interests that we have faced several times this century. But I do believe that the problem is a serious one, much like an epidemic or a famine, that if unchecked can seriously undermine the broader goals that we as a nation have set for ourselves. Awareness is critical, an awareness that crime is not simply a matter of individual violence or threat or a slightly romanticized activity engaged in by colorful characters in the movies. It is, or if unchecked can be, a profoundly corrupting force.

The risks involved in failing to appreciate these issues is great. Journalist Steve Handelman writing in *Foreign Affairs* last spring noted that part of the rapid growth of the Russian Mafia was due to Russia's "seeking to develop a free market before constructing a civil society in which such a market could safely operate." That observation is equally true about maintaining civil society elsewhere in the world. That is why CSIS, I believe, deserves a very special thanks for seeking to focus attention on these issues and why I am so grateful to have had the opportunity to share these thoughts with you.

Question and Answer Session

William Colby: About six or eight weeks ago, the leaders of the Cali cartel got together with some of their "patron saints" who helped set them up in business back when they were not so powerful. The subject of the meeting was not how to infiltrate business and how to establish better control of business in Colombia or elsewhere. They felt they had a pretty good handle on that. The subject of the meeting was how to more effectively control the Colombian government. They already had significant assets in the Congress. They had put money into the presidential campaign to ensure cooperation from the highest levels of the Colombian government that was incoming at the time.

What they were planning to do and what they are hoping to implement is better ways of manipulating the government in order to facilitate the protection of their activities, their penetration, and also to deal with the kinds of enforcement environment that you are talking about in international cooperation—whether it is through the Financial Action Task Force or others.

We know what is happening in Russia and the kinds of problems the Russian government is having. We have seen what has happened in Italy. One of the things we have not talked about so far in this meeting is the activities of Asian organized crime and its ability to penetrate governments in various parts of the world and manipulate them. It seems to me that, in the environment that we are talking about, we are not just talking about the penetration of the business and financial community, but the ability of criminal organizations—especially the large ones increasingly—to influence, penetrate, and corrupt governments.

Would you care to comment on the kinds of things that we might do in this area in order to try to deal with that kind of problem?

Mr. Morris: The observation is apt and eloquently put. The only comment I would make is that I think that, clearly, organized criminal activity is the greatest destabilizing influence in terms of a lot of nascent democratic governments around the world. It is why, it seems to me, dealing with it has to be a central part of our foreign policy.

The only observation I can make is that, as you build a new country, it is very important to try to maintain the integrity of your financial system, because that is how criminal enterprises basically develop economic power. They begin to penetrate not just the criminal activity—whether it is extortion, prostitution, drugs, or whatever—but also the legitimate aspects of the economy. Then they have economic power, and, as we all know from Political Science 1A, economic power is almost directly attributable to political power. So, I think that that does not demean the importance of trying to focus across the board.

The other observation I would make—and I feel it very, very strongly—is that there is no simple, easy answer to what is, in fact, a very complex problem. The worst thing, it would seem to me, is to view this as something the cops do. "We're going to solve this. We're going to put two FBI agents in Moscow and that will fix that. We'll give FinCEN a new computer." That will not solve it. It will not even barely address it. What has to really be done is that we as a matter of fundamental national policy have to address this across the board. Then we need to engage the people who really know something about money, and that is the financial community, as allies.

Mr. de Borchgrave: Mr. Morris, can I ask you how, in your judgment, one could streamline the 32 agencies currently involved in Washington in coping with global organized crime? I believe it is 32. It could be 35. Could it be cut down to five or six, and how would you go about it?

Mr. Morris: I am not a big believer in moving boxes around organizationally. There are advantages to specialized skills. I have always thought—and Judge Webster and I have talked about this on a number of occasions—that what you have to do is change the measures of performance, change the measures of success. If you measure cooperation, if you take two steps back to avoid what are the simple, easy measures, you can encourage cooperation across bureaucratic lines.

Anybody who has ever run a large organization, or even a small organization, finds bureaucratic battles within their own organization. You know, in Customs—I have Carol Hallett looking right at me here—you always have the tension between the enforcement and civil sections. At FinCEN, you have the tensions between the enforcement gun-toters and the intelligence analysts and all. It would seem to me that we need to raise the level of how we measure their performance and build that into how we manage the organizations, because there is value to the skills that you have. You cannot simply say we are going to have one great large agency that will handle everything from counterfeiting to trade fraud to all of the rest. Then you are just going to end up with one great big large organization and, in some ways, probably not as constructive an organization.

I do not think the numbers are so important. I think it is the way that we have to engage the people working in those organizations to see that, individually, nobody can deal with this issue and that clear cooperation and partnership is what gets rewarded. We try to get out of what are the easy measures.

Question: Mr. Morris, one of the things that they talked about quite a bit today was how money flowed around the world via wire transfers. But one of the things that I think has been generally neglected is how much U.S. currency has become the sort of worldwide transmitter of wealth both for legitimate and illegitimate channels.

I was wondering if that was one of the measures of performance in terms of what you could do about tracking, having established baselines, to guide other agencies as they move down the investigative paths so you could make more strategic interventions?

Mr. Morris: The answer is yes. We have been very much interested in trying to understand what currency flows really mean. One passing observation I would make, and I have just discovered this recently, that is that there has been very little market in the right places for strategic intelligence. I have heard DEA complain about the CIA's products, "they give us these pretty maps," but DEA does not care about the pretty maps. What DEA really cares about is where the bad guy is at what particular time so that they can do what they do, which is arrest him, seize his property, his plane or, you know, make a case.

What I have discovered—and maybe many of you have probably known this a long time—is that now, at least within my little world in the anti-money laundering center at Treasury, there is a key interest in strategic intelligence, not for the law enforcement agency but to design the compliance programs for the banks who want to know and to design the regulatory schemes. So often we have, I think, basically been trying to take a product, quality strategic intelligence, and sell it to the wrong people.

I think that, yes, there is clearly a need to understand what is going on. But we need to make sure that we are developing products that have some utility to the real users. I think too often there may have been a slip between the cup and the lip there.

Mr. Bloom: Mike Bloom from Planning Management Analysis at Treasury.

There is a lot of congressional interest these days in performance measurement of the Government Performance and Results Act, the CFO Act. All those require measures. You mentioned that you believe there is no architecture in place right now for measurement of things like enforcement and prevention. We have been trying at Treasury, as you know, to work on impact or outcome measures with an opportunity for law enforcement groups to explain a number that may look a little strange.

Are there any other ideas you have on the directions law enforcement can take in measuring the types of activities that you are talking about and getting at the prevention, getting at the enforcement, to satisfy Congress and the public that action is being taken appropriately?

Mr. Morris: Mike, you really ask hard questions. That is probably the $64,000 one. You cannot have a performance measure at all unless you have a fairly sound understanding of the problem that you are trying to address. I do not think, as it relates to organized crime, we have really got that sophisticated a definition of the problem. I do not think that that problem definition can come from an organization that has, as I said in my remarks, a solution in mind. Because, if your solution is to increase arrest, you will define the problem by that. Whatever you start with your solution, that drives the nature of your problem.

I think a conference like this that cuts across enforcement, intelligence, business, and regulators is very valuable because it has to assault some of our preconceptions. Once you have identified the problem at the most macro level, which is what policy leaders ought to have, and you develop some of that strategic intelligence that we really have not done very well by—at least in my organization, then you can define the problem. Then you can begin to develop the necessary measures to determine how you are doing against it. But, too often, I think, we take too narrow a view of the problem, and that is based, to some extent, on the reality that people do view issues parochially, based upon what their tools are. Where you stand depends on where you sit—the classic truism of Washington.

Mr. Federmann: Do you believe there is a correlation between the decline of the dollar on international currency markets and the fact that the dollar became the unit of all black business in the world? It is very dangerous for the United States if it has.

Mr. Morris: The reality is that the U.S. dollar, of course, is still the major currency in the world in which transactions are carried out. That is a truism. I do not think it would make much difference if we went to the mark or the yen or something else. The issue would remain the same. I also know that there has been some discussion earlier about ways of changing the color of the currency. Not wanting to get into the middle of such a debate, I have some suspicions. As Mencken once said, "for every complex, difficult problem, there's an easy, short, low-cost solution that's wrong." My own sense is that we already discount dirty money. Indeed, if you look at the impact of what it costs to launder money in the communities in the United States, it has nearly doubled in the last five years. Whereas the price of dope has been pretty much the same. Our regulatory and enforcement effort as it relates to money laundering has increased that cost, but it is discounted. Today, if you were going to launder money in Miami, you would probably be paying 10 or 12 percent. A few years ago, you were paying 5 or 6 percent. If you change the color of the currency, you would have a one-time shot, and it would increase the cost of laundering that dirty money maybe to 20 percent. So, you would affect the profit margins by some marginal amount. Whether that is worth it or not I will leave for the policymakers to decide.

Crooks are going to exchange whatever crooks are going to exchange and whatever works for them in whatever markets are effective. I do not think it is necessarily material that it happens to be the U.S. dollar in large parts of the world. What drives a lot of it, of course, is our insatiable drug habit in this country, which does flush lots of money. Beyond that, crooks are going to negotiate in whatever means are necessary to pay bills, buy assets, and that sort of thing.

The International Black Market: Coping with Drugs, Thugs, and Fissile Materials

Ambassador Carol Hallett, Chair
Commissioner, U.S. Customs Service (Ret.)

Mr. de Borchgrave: We are now in the anomalous position in which legitimate multinational business activity is being rivaled by an equally robust worldwide illegitimate business establishment. There is nothing new, as we all know, about trafficking in drugs and arms, or people for that matter.

What is new is that weapons of mass destruction are becoming available in the underground marketplace. What is also new is that the criminal underground is interconnected globally in ways that we have never seen, as demonstrated by earlier panels. Most important of all, I think, is the fact that global criminals armed with billions of dollars are corrupting legitimate economic, social, and political institutions.

In the chair is a most remarkable woman I have had the privilege of knowing for many years, Ambassador Carol Hallett. As commissioner of Customs, Ambassador Hallett was the nation's highest ranking female law enforcement official—that is, before Janet Reno—and directed some 20,000 employees, generated $20 billion a year in revenue, and processed over $1 trillion in trade, two-way trade, annually. I know she was responsible for the landmark DEA-Customs Agreement that gave Customs' special agents full investigative authority for narcotics and money laundering.

She is also the only woman I know—probably there are several more by now—but as far as I know, she is the only woman who was fully checked out on the three most advanced fighter aircraft that we possess. She is a great pilot. As ambassador to the Bahamas, I was also familiar with her work down there. She is the woman who actually busted the connection between the then government of the Bahamas and the Medellín cartel.

Dr. Rensselaer Lee, who also speaks Russian, Chinese, Spanish, and French, is an expert's expert who has testified before countless congressional committees and has appeared repeatedly on our TV networks' principal news and magazine programs. He has written extensively on narcotics, transnational crime, and political change in

Eurasia and Latin America. He is the author of *The White Labyrinth: Cocaine and Political Power* and is now finishing a book on organized crime and its political connections in the former Soviet Union. Dr. Lee is president of Global Advisory Services, a firm based across the river in Alexandria, that consults in all these interrelated fields for the U.S. government and for multinational corporations.

Buck Revell became a legend in his 30 years with the FBI, where he directed the Bureau's programs on organized crime and was serving as the director's principal deputy for criminal investigations, counterterrorism, and counterintelligence activities when I first had the privilege of meeting him.

He was responsible for all international investigative liaison activities, including Interpol, was a member of the National Foreign Intelligence Board, the Terrorist Crisis Management Center, the Deputy's Committee of the National Security Council, and was given command of a joint FBI/CIA military operation, Operation Goldenrod, which lead to the first apprehension overseas of an international terrorist. After numerous awards for meritorious service, Judge William Webster, then the DCI, gave Buck the National Intelligence Distinguished Service Medal.

Dr. David Kay you all remember. David was familiar to millions of TV viewers all over the world as he demonstrated a bulldog tenacity in leading UN nuclear weapons inspections in post-Gulf War Iraq. The proliferation and counterproliferation of weapons of mass destruction is a field he has testified about frequently before Congress. His writings on nuclear and defense matters in the 25 states that have some form of nuclear ambitions have appeared in leading publications here and abroad. He is now vice president for Planning at the Science Applications International Corporation.

Ambassador Hallett, you are cleared for takeoff.

Carol Hallett

I think, first of all, it is really appropriate to compliment CSIS and particularly Judge Webster and Arnaud de Borchgrave for the phenomenal production that has taken place today. This is not easy. It has been already most informative, and I think each one of you would agree that, while to a certain extent some of us may be preaching to the choir, we are nevertheless making a tremendous impact in coming up with information and sharing that is going to be invaluable in setting the stage for how we deal with these very serious problems in the future.

When it comes to coping with drugs, thugs, and nuclear missiles, our panel title in and of itself says a lot. But what it does not say is that there is truly a linkage between world organized crime groups and one other key and very important way of doing business. That is networking. All of us have been told over the many years that to be successful you must be able to network.

Well, historically, I guess the one group of people who have successfully networked have been the Mafia groups. Whether it has been the Mafia itself, the Cosa Nostra, whether it has been the Chinese Tongs, or, certainly, whether it has been the Japanese Yakuza, or any other group, they have been successful because they have networked and networked with one another. These groups have traditionally been able to operate not only within their own local areas, but also throughout national spheres of influence. By the 1980s and the 1990s, we were able to identify a very significant shift from what had previously been a way of doing business to more interactive relationships. As we have seen, there was now an effort to try and reach out to the Colombian cartels. And the Colombian cartels started reaching out to those cartels in Mexico as a way of doing business and moving drugs into the United States.

As we saw this taking place, we were very slow in many instances to react. One of the reasons is because these bad guys are guerrillas in the way they operate. We, of course, are the regular army and, so, we have to do things with not only a built-in budget but also rules and regulations that control and keep us from doing anything out of the norm. Meanwhile, we had the bad guys—the Mafia, all of the Columbian cartels, all of the other drug-related and non-drug-related organizations—literally freewheeling it with no budget constraints, nothing to keep them in tow other than the tremendous effort being put forth primarily by U.S. law enforcement agencies. This being the case, we had twice the job to do, with, obviously, a very small amount of money in comparison to what those organizations have and will have in the foreseeable future.

One of the areas where we have a very significant problem is the movement of money, not only through wire systems but many other systems. And of course, the cartels and the Mafia have for years had as their number one way of doing business the ability to move money around. One of the problems that we have always been confronted with is how do we stop them?

I think Senator Leahy's efforts to try and change not only the $100 bill but also put pressure on these individuals who traffic money is truly one of the most important steps in the right direction. Because, while it may be a one-time shot, as was suggested by Stan Morris, it is nevertheless disruptive. And, every time we are able to disrupt the cartels or the bad guys we make progress. Disruption will continue to be one of the most important ways that we can have an impact on what is going on a worldwide basis.

Let me give you an example of a very disruptive but very successful event that took place on my watch in 1992. It was, in fact, the ability to bring down a money laundering organization that was operating between Miami and New York. In a very sophisticated and a very successful undercover operation, customs put together the means by which we would be able as a business to theoretically launder money for an organization that had been highly successful in moving their money in and out of the United States. By the time we took that organization down, we had seized $22 million in cash. The catch to this is that it was all in $1, $5, $10, and $20 bills. $11 million of it was in $10 bills.

Now, why do I share this with you? The reason is that, because no matter what mechanism the drug traffickers utilize, they are hopelessly lost unless they are able to launder their money. We are talking about the big organizations laundering $100 bills. What we have to also keep in mind is that, if we are really going to succeed in beating these people, we must stop them from laundering the street money. Of those dollars, $11 million was in $10 bills, worthless money. Over $2 million of those dollars was in $1 bills. You might as well have a bonfire and burn that money unless you can get rid of it. That is one of the reasons why it is going to be so critically important for us to come up with even newer mechanisms and ways in which we are able to stop not only the drug traffickers but all of the other people who are in business for one reason only to make money illegally. We must cut off their ability to launder those proceeds.

I do not think I have heard the figures mentioned this morning across the board. But let us just keep in mind that it is estimated that about $100 billion is laundered yearly in the United States. Worldwide, $300 to $500 billion is laundered annually. What most people do not realize is that 60 to 70 percent of that money is non-drug-related. And, so, with all of the various criminal operations going on out there, we many times lose focus. The money can be from arms; it can be from illegal or clandestine trade—something as simple as moving goods and textiles in from China, not only changing the country of origin, but changing the quota numbers by transshipping those goods through another country. So too, we will see a scheme in which those countries or companies can launder money that would otherwise be useless to them.

When we take a look at this and realize that in the United States, in Canada, in Europe, and in any country around us, whether it is Mexico, or whether it is South American or Asian countries, one thing is sure. All of these illegal organizations, have, again, one thing in common: the sharing of information and the ability to continue to make money.

Canada is a good example of a country where illicit drug trade is, in fact, the largest single source of revenue for organized crime. Most people do not even think of Canada as having the drug trade as their single largest source of illegal funds. But it is. One of the things that has been very successful for those organizations in Canada is they are able to easily move money as well as drugs in and out of the northeast of the

United States. Too often we lose focus and think everything is coming the easy way, through the Bahamas or through Mexico, or through some other countries south of us, when in fact, much of the problem has been related to those drugs that have been transshipped direct to Canada and then moved back into the United States.

Whether it is the problem we have in North America or whether it is the problem we have around the world, one of the areas we are going to hear more about today and on which we need to spend more time is how are we going to deal with all of these countries, bringing them together, so that we can reach agreement with respect to the sharing of information.

There is no question that connectibility, the networking of all of the groups that are out there, is going to be critical. We have to find ways to deal with not only what the last panel today spoke about, the success of the computerized networks today. That is a way of communication. Just keep in mind that the traffickers as well as all of the money launderers are going to fail if they are unable to communicate. That means, in addition to the utilization of computers, they are totally dependent upon faxes, phones, and the mail system.

We must devise more ways not only in the United States but around the world to curtail their ability to utilize those systems. They have physical meetings. The next thing we know, they are going to have televised meetings with one another, literally taking place as we sit in this room. We have to worry more and more about the electronic transfer of funds. And while it is true what Stan said, whether it is a Casa de Cambio or whether it is simply going to a place where people get money orders in order to launder those funds, it is going to continue to be a focus for law enforcement if we are going to be able to make those changes and stop this illegal activity.

What about visas and travel? There is another area where we can have a greater impact, along with the business of finding out all of these banking records and being able to have even greater controls over the banks and their ability to accept dirty money. How many of you realize that, if we are going to be able to disrupt their activities, then we are going to have to have a singular system where information is gathered on a worldwide basis? Then we also have to be able to depend on a level of trust and credibility on a worldwide basis that that information, which is gathered and shared, is not going to end up back in the hands of those who are carrying on illegal activities.

Yes, we need to operate against the criminal elements on a worldwide basis. But, just as an example, if you were to look at custom services around the world, one thing you would find almost universally, with the exception of three or four, is that every single one of their enforcement people is underpaid. They make up that loss of money that their counterparts in some other agency might be making by, of course, getting involved in illegal activities.

A good example is what has happened in Nigeria with the customs service there. You do not have to be a member of the customs service to go out and buy a customs uniform and then appear at a border crossing or appear at an airport. It is simply whatever monies you can make off of the goods coming into that country that are yours, wearing your customs uniform. These are frightening problems that I am sure are perpetuated on a worldwide basis. Whether it is a law enforcement organization or any other organization, it is not a simple process of being able to cooperate, being able to share, and then being able to depend on those individuals with whom you are working to keep all of that information in legal, honest channels.

One of the things that drives all of this is the continuing ability of the bad guys to go to certain countries and be able to continue to keep their criminal organizations going because they know they can launder their money in these locations. Stan Morris alluded to it; others have alluded to it. But the bottom line is that, as long as we have places like those mentioned today—the Cayman Islands, the Turks and Caicos, the British Virgin Islands, just to name a few, then we have an uphill battle. But remember this, those three examples are not independent nations. They are under the United Kingdom. Do we get tough with the governor general of the Cayman Islands, or do we get tough with those individuals in the UK who are responsible for appointing the governor general of the Turks and Caicos or the Cayman Islands? These are tough questions that we are going to have to start dealing with at a national level. I think when we do, and I think when we come down even much harder, we will find it will make a difference.

This morning, the question was asked about how we are going to be able to get more countries to cooperate. The fact of the matter is, under the G-7—and this is, in fact, something that was orchestrated by Jim Baker during his tenure as the secretary of the treasury—they were actually able through the G-7 to build an agreement with international organizations based in Paris, an agreement whereby we actually are now able to get greater control and greater cooperation with some 26 different countries that have all signed such an agreement. The agreement is fine unless, of course, the information is shared with those people who are not going to be able to treat it in an ethical manner.

But the bottom line is that when you take one step further and you look at the former Soviet Union, those FSU states are still today using dollars because they cannot use credit cards. What are you going to do? You have got a problem no matter where you go. We are going to have to spend much more time in reality if we are going to be able to bring this whole issue to the forefront.

Certainly, this week is the most ideal week for this conference to be taking place.

With the summit between Presidents Clinton and Yeltsin, one of the highest issues on the agenda must be international organized crime, particularly as it relates to those issues that our distinguished panel is going to be discussing today: whether it is the proliferation of nuclear materials; whether it is simply weapons such as AK-47s or any other kinds of weapons that are coming out of the former Soviet Union; or whether it is the very startling and very worrisome problem that is also continuing to develop in the old Soviet Union (and now, of course, in central Europe)—the growth of narcotics and the transportation of narcotics through those countries.

One of the things that was not mentioned today with respect to that one ton of cocaine that was recently seized going into Vyborg was the fact that it was concealed. It was not in open containers or in open packages of cocaine. It was one ton of cocaine concealed in cans that were labeled "meat" and "potatoes." No matter where you go in the world today, the schemes are the same; the problems are the same. We must just find ways in which we will be able to zero in on these problems and come up with solutions.

That is what CSIS is doing today with this conference. That is what CSIS will continue to do—come up with recommended solutions that will help us get a handle on what can otherwise be the single biggest threat to the security of not just our country but to all democracies throughout the world. That is why I think that our panel today is one in which many of the questions that we are concerned about are going to be answered.

We are going to start the panel today with Dr. Lee, who is going to concentrate his comments primarily on what is going on in the FSU and what we can prepare do in the years and, certainly, the days ahead.

Rensselaer Lee

The end of the cold war, as you all know, has been a wonderful thing. It has meant the end of direct East-West military confrontation in Europe, the opening of borders to the West, and trade, commercial relations, and a redefinition of the U.S.-Russian relationship to stress the ideal of partnership in world affairs. That is the good news.

Unfortunately, the demise of communism in Russia and other countries has created an array of very new and very dangerous security threats to the West. Many of these threats are associated with criminal affluence of various kinds from the decayed Soviet empire, including trafficking in narcotics, weapons, radioactive materials, body parts, prostitutes, illegal aliens, computer viruses, counterfeit money—just to name a few. Also, we are now faced with the wholesale transplantation of Russian criminal groups to various western countries, where they are engaging in many of the same kinds of rackets that they were involved in their own country.

In short, although the empire is more or less dead, in theory at least, the empire seems to be striking back in unforeseen and very unpleasant ways. Now, a particularly alarming form of criminality associated with the Soviet Union's collapse has been the soaring illegal trade in radioactive materials—in uranium, plutonium, cesium, strontium, and cobalt 60. Various different kinds of materials now are coming out of the former Soviet Union. This is the problem that I want to talk about mostly today.

There have been literally hundreds of thefts of such substances at nuclear institutes and enterprises around the former Soviet Union during the 1990s. If you look at the statistics of the German Federal Police, the Bundeskriminalamt, they reported about 200 to 300 apparently genuine attempts to sell nuclear materials in Germany since 1992. There have also been more than 40 seizures in Germany over the last two or three years. Also, although Germany seems to be on the cutting edge of this problem, really these materials are spreading around to other countries in Europe, for example, to Italy, Czechoslovakia, Poland, Austria, Romania, and Turkey. Turkey is possibly an entrepot for the movement of nuclear materials into the Arab world in the Middle East.

Now, most of the nuclear materials that are appearing in international black markets so far consist of low-grade uranium and of radioactive isotopes such as cesium 137 and strontium 90. Although they are environmentally hazardous substances, to be sure, they cannot really be used to make ordinary types of nuclear weapons. But the quality of stolen and smuggled substances is definitely improving.

You will recall that this year, between May and August, German authorities confiscated a couple of significant shipments of Plutonium-239, as well as a quantity of weapons-grade uranium. In Russia, multikilogram quantities of weapons-usable uranium were stolen in 1993 and 1994 from a Ministry of Atomic Energy fuel complex near Moscow and also, perhaps more worrisome, from a submarine fuel depot in the northern fleet base in Murmansk, in northern Russia. Obviously, this is a business that bears watching. It has a number of very dangerous aspects, and Western police, security, and intelligence agencies have got to prepare themselves for an increasing influx of dangerous radioactive materials coming from the East.

I think it is a legitimate question as we try to look at the anatomy of this trade. We have got to figure out what factors appear to be prompting this rising traffic in nuclear radioactive materials. Here, we can trot out a number of explanations: certainly the general disintegration of Communist control structures, the chaos in these systems that were in that part of the world, the stream of privatization, defense conversion, economic and political uncertainty, and the transparency of borders. All of these factors are contributing to this general problem. But I would say, certainly from my observations, that the principal cause lies in the conditions in the civilian and defense nuclear enterprises themselves.

It is very clear, I think, to everybody who has observed and studied this problem that the physical security of many of these institutions has deteriorated. The guard forces on the perimeters of these enterprises are often corrupt. Radioactive monitors do not work very well. The Russians simply lack the means to monitor their huge inventories of enriched uranium and plutonium. The down-sizing of the nuclear complex also has had a catastrophic effect on employees' well-being and morale.

Nuclear scientists, formerly the cream of Soviet society, have seen their fortunes suffer a complete reversal over a short period of years. Some of these people are being paid as little as $10 a month. You have delays in payment of wages and salaries; these are common. Sometimes people wait as long as four months in some enterprises before receiving pay checks. There are reports of strikes and work stoppages in several of Russia's formerly "secret" cities. Aggravating this problem is the publication in Russian and also in western media of reports of fabulous, hypothetical prices to be realized from selling enriched uranium, plutonium, and other radioactive materials on international black markets. So, it is not surprising that people reading these reports, suffering terrible economic privations, and very angry at their reversal in status from the Soviet period, that people are stealing and trying to peddle these substances in large numbers.

I do not want to sound unduly alarmist on this topic. I think there has been some problem with the way the mass media has handled the problem of nuclear trafficking. It is not quite as horrific a phenomenon as it has been depicted in some European and U.S. news media. The nuclear trade is clearly not really like other illegal businesses and I think almost everybody who has looked at it agrees. It is not like the drug business, for example. It is not like smuggling weapons. It is not like most other illegal businesses. It is principally a supply-driven business, and the suppliers, of course, are these disgruntled, angry, and economically desperate employees, or former employees, of nuclear enterprises.

Also, trading and marketing opportunities for nuclear substances tend to be fairly narrow. There simply are not that many people who deal in these substances. Legitimate buyers—and I think this is the main point—are very few and far between. In Europe, the buyers do not seem to be the North Koreans, the Iraqis, the Pakistanis, and the Iranians that we would expect to see out there. At least law enforcement officials in European countries have not been able to establish connections with people of these nationalities very conclusively. Rather, the market for nuclear substances appears to be composed of an assortment of police, undercover agents, intelligence operatives, and journalists.

For example, the large 300-gram plutonium shipment from Moscow that was seized in Munich last August was really the product of an elaborate sting operation involving the Bavarian police and the German Intelligence Service and a few criminals. The Germans had made a deal with some of these criminals to buy maybe four, maybe seven kilograms of plutonium for about $250 million. So, these guys had these discussions in Germany in July. In August, they went to Moscow, and they got hold of the plutonium. They brought it back to Munich—some of it, 300 or 350 grams—and this, apparently, was the first batch or installment of this deal. And then the criminals were arrested.

I also read in a Russian newspaper that a German citizen arrested in Bremen last August for trying to sell microgram quantities of plutonium was, in fact, a police agent for the Land Department of Criminal Affairs of Bremen, and his buyer was an agent of the Land Department of Criminal Affairs of Hamburg. Both were working on nuclear smuggling cases and, somehow, they tripped over each other. Maybe my German friends will correct me if I am wrong on this. I cannot say that there is no black market out there for nuclear materials, but I think to the extent that the market exists, the market is pretty thin even for so-called weapons-usable materials.

Now, because of the rather peculiar characteristics of the illegal nuclear trade, Russia's established criminal organizations so far, by most indications at least, have shown very little interest in the radioactive materials traffic. This, I guess, is fortunate in a way. It is fortunate in a way for the wrong reasons, because organized crime's main businesses—extortion rackets, narcotics, car theft, financial fraud, and contraband raw material exports—are so profitable that, in a way, criminal groups are rather satisfied doing the things that they are doing now. By contrast, a very high profile, risky, and uncertain business like nuclear trafficking might well be unattractive to most professional criminals. I think this is true of the major established Russian organized crime groups. It may also be true of groups such as the Medellín or Cali cartels, or possibly some of the Italian organized crime groups.

But we cannot discount the possibility that specialized nuclear trading networks (you might say a new class of nuclear criminals, unrelated to existing organized crime formations), might emerge at some time in the future. More ominously, existing patterns of nuclear theft and smuggling may simply be setting the stage or laying the ground work for far more serious proliferation episodes in the future, for example, the large-scale illegal exports of weapons-grade fissile materials, or even of finished nuclear weapons.

Certainly, I think the closing off of the smuggling channels and improving nuclear safety at enterprises is going to require an unprecedented level of U.S.-Russian cooperation and probably a very significant influx of U.S. technical and economic assistance. Unfortunately, Russian officials are resistant to having a serious dialogue on the nuclear crime issue. Indeed, there is a tendency on the part of Russian officials to see the entire issue as a smoke screen for Western schemes aimed at penetrating and controlling Russia's nuclear defense establishment. I think that this, what I would call a paranoid and ostrich-like stance on the part of Moscow bureaucrats, is really, in a way, reminiscent of the worst days of the cold war.

Oliver "Buck" Revell

This is indeed an intriguing conference for me, having spent the last 30 years of my life in this business. To see this level of interest and concern, I think, is very, very important. I join in extending my appreciation to CSIS for taking on this topic.

I want to discuss two models based upon the experience that we have had over the past 15 years or so. I will try to dissect the difference in the results and perhaps the methods by which they came about to provide some insight on how we ought to approach this whole phenomenon.

Back in 1982, Director Webster was in charge of the Bureau. We acquired concurrent drug jurisdiction with the DEA and set about trying to use some of the tools and techniques that the FBI had honed against the Mafia, La Cosa Nostra, in the United States to go after major drug cartels.

In October of 1982, with Director Webster's approval, we convened a conference at Quantico, which we named, somewhat uniquely, the Quantico Working Group. Participating in this conference were the Royal Canadian Mounted Police, the Australian Federal Police, and a large delegation of Italians: the Italian State Police, the Carabinieri, the Guardia di Finanza, the high commissioner against the Mafia, and several investigative magistrates assigned to investigate the Mafia, including Giovanni Falcone. We gathered to discuss a particular phenomenon, Italian organized crime with American and Canadian counterparts and their involvement in, particularly, heroin trafficking. It was an area that we knew was increasing, but we were not certain as to its extent.

During this very informal, two-day exchange, we found that the Canadians and the Australians knew a great deal about what was happening in the United States. We certainly knew what was happening in the United States to some extent, but all of us found that we learned something new, including the fact that we had a whole infrastructure and apparatus operating in the United States that had not heretofore been specifically identified. We thought that all organized crime of the Italian type in the United States would be under the auspices of La Cosa Nostra. We soon found out in comparing notes that that was not the case.

We had an entirely independent set of primarily Sicilian Mafia but also some Camorra members that were operating in the United States independent of La Cosa

Nostra. We also found out that the 'Ndrangheta, another Italian group, was operating very substantially in Canada. We decided to agree to continue the working group process and informal exchanges to try and improve our capability to deal with these types of evolving phenomena.

In January of 1984, some 15 months after the first meeting, we met in Ottawa, Canada. The players and the scope of the conference expanded, and we got into specific cases. The scope of the Sicilian Mafia infiltration into North America was explored in depth. A cooperative relationship was required to pursue these new revelations.

Out of this particular conference and the case discussions and the exchange of information from some recently developed informants—including a very high level informant that DEA had developed inside the Sicilian Mafia, we were able to predicate a series of cases that in the United States became known as the Pizza Connection cases. "Pizza Connection II" only occurred a few weeks ago. Ultimately, much of this information found its way back into the Italian criminal justice arena and resulted in the predicate and eventually in the ultimate trial, the maxi-trial, in Italy itself. We established joint databases and agreed to the exchange of law enforcement operational—not liaison but operational—personnel, which was a unique circumstance.

In early 1985, the Italians were due to host the Quantico Working Group, and the Italian State Police went to the minister of interior, Oscar Luigi Scarfo. Minister Scarfo was so taken with this process he decided to host the conference. Our attorney general at the time, William French Smith, and Director Webster decided that, if the minister of interior was going to host the conference, they certainly should participate, and, indeed, they did. In fact, the result of the conference was that there was such an outstanding degree of information exchange and camaraderie that developed around this particular theme that the working group was escalated to the cabinet level.

The group continued to evolve and develop. After the Achilles Lauro incident, which was very traumatic for our Italian counterparts, terrorism was added to the agenda. Out of this working process at the cabinet- and working-level came an MLAT, a revised extradition treaty, and an ongoing working relationship. The Italian government undertook many reforms and, if Claire Sterling is correct, they may not hold. But, at least we saw for the first time the diminution of the power of the Mafia over the activities of Italian commerce and, to some extent, its government.

We tried to apply those same lessons on a broader basis in Trevi (an organization of European ministers of justice and interior associated with the European community). Director Webster became active in Trevi as was Attorney General William French Smith, Ed Meese, and so forth. When Director Sessions came in, he immediately started participating in the Trevi process, and we became involved in many of the same issues.

Let me turn to another country that is much closer to home and with which the developments have not been quite as positive and dramatic, and that is Mexico. We share a 2,000 mile border with Mexico. We share a common heritage in that we were both colonies. We have a tremendous number of people of Mexican heritage within the United States. Our businesses have a great deal of investment in Mexico and vice versa. We have every reason to have a strong and supportive relationship, and in many ways we do.

But as the NAFTA Treaty was being negotiated, there was not one mention of the difficulties that we have at the legal level, at the law enforcement level. We have no extradition treaty with Mexico; we have no mutual legal assistance treaty with Mexico, and, in fact, we have had a great many problems with the level of corruption within law enforcement in Mexico. In 1982, the FBI in San Diego indicted the director of the Federales in a sting operation. In 1986, the chief of their National Central Bureau committed suicide after we had implicated him in significant drug smuggling activities. We have not reached the level where we have a common trust or bond with law enforcement—even though we have tried through exchanges and through training and so forth–essentially because the Mexican law enforcement model has not come up to the level of ethics and standards that allows us to have this sort of continuing relationship.

Now, does this make a difference? Well, coming out of Texas, let me tell you what has happened over the past five years. We have found that more than 80 percent of the drugs in Texas come from Mexico, which is no big surprise. We have also found that the street gangs in Dallas and Fort Worth and Houston are being supplied by the Mexican Mafia. If they are black street gangs, they are being supplied many times by Jamaican posses who are getting the drugs from the Mexican Mafia. There is a direct correlation between our ability to engage in appropriate law enforcement activity with the Mexican authorities and the ability to shut off contraband coming from Mexico and shut off other types of criminal activities across the border.

The first and foremost significant impediment to effective enforcement is the lack of cooperative relationships between nations at the political and legal level. Many countries in which organized crime is prevalent either do not have effective extradition treaties with the United States or in certain instances, there are no treaties at all. The lack of mutual legal assistance treaties is also a significant barrier to effective law enforcement cooperation. To make matters worse, a significant number of countries with which the United States has substantial economic activity have enacted stringent bank secrecy acts, providing an almost impenetrable barrier to international law enforcement. By the very nature of the bank secrecy activities of such countries, they become facilitators for international organized crime, drug trafficking, money laundering, and fraud. The government of the United States should insist that these protective barriers be lowered for legitimate law enforcement purposes or the U.S. government will unilaterally, if necessary, invoke significant economic sanctions against the offending nation.

The United States should not enter into trade agreements or other economic treaties with a nation without a full assessment of the law enforcement impact of such a relationship. At the very least, extradition and mutual legal assistance treaties ought to be in place before foreign nations are given virtually free access to U.S. markets. In the NAFTA, there were no law enforcement considerations. Senior law enforcement officials were also instructed not to raise issues or objections in regard to the treaty. The United States Senate, however, should not confirm any treaty or trade agreement that does not provide adequate legal protection for U.S. citizens and require that law enforcement and judicial procedures adequate to protect U.S. interests are either in place or include within the treaty provisions.

The second major impediment to effective enforcement is the lack of control of our own borders. We have recently experienced a second round of indictments and arrests of Sicilian Mafia members operating substantial drug trafficking organizations in the United States, independent of the American La Cosa Nostra. This case is commonly known as the "Pizza Connection II." Throughout the Southwest, Mexican Mafia groups, most of whom are in the United States illegally, are operating significant drug trafficking organizations and providing street gangs with drugs and guns, thereby increasing the level of violent crime on our streets. The same is true of Jamaican Posse organizations and Nigerian criminal groups. The vast majority of the membership of these criminal enterprises are in the United States illegally, either through subterfuge, forged documents, or illicit entry across our borders. In addition, many organized criminals have entered the United States through false claims for political asylum thereafter to disappear into the various criminal networks operating within the United States. The federal government has never demonstrated either the will or determination to adequately control our borders to stop the criminal trafficking in illicit goods and illegal aliens.

Increasing technology available to criminal elements is another significant impediment to effective enforcement against organized criminal groups. Without the electronic surveillance provisions of the Organized Crime & Safe Streets Act of 1968, the FBI and other federal enforcement agencies would not have been able to attack and reduce organized crime, terrorism, and drug trafficking to anywhere near the extent that has been accomplished to date. If we are to protect the citizens, financial institutions, and the integrity of government of our nation, then an answer must be found to the Digital Telephony and Optical Technology issues. If organized criminal groups are able to use our information highway with impunity, then sophisticated criminal activities will proliferate at a significantly accelerating rate.

Finally, I believe it is absolutely essential that there be wholesale sharing of intelligence by U.S. law enforcement and intelligence agencies. There was tremendous opposition and intransigence in the position of numerous agencies to the creation of the National Drugs Intelligence Center (NDIC). In 1985, when I first proposed the creation of the NDIC to then FBI Director Webster, the DEA opposed the creation of an all-source national intelligence center, and since then there has been little improvement in the interagency intelligence sharing process. What is needed is a presidential directive requiring all federal agencies, whether law enforcement, intelligence, or regulatory, to report and/or furnish all pertinent information to a newly established national criminal intelligence center. Such a center would enable the federal government and its various components to develop a strategic approach to combating major international crime and criminal enterprise organizations. The current system of separation of responsibility among numerous agencies and a lack of meaningful coordination simply gives the criminal element and advantage that we cannot afford. If Russian, Italian, Colombian, and American organized crime groups can establish cooperative relations and joint ventures, then surely we should be able to create a productive relationship between our enforcement, intelligence, and regulatory agencies to combat this growing threat.

David Kay

What I would like to do today is talk briefly about what I view as the preeminent national security threat for the next generation of Americans. I say this because I believe that we have survived almost 50 years of nuclear weapons because they, in fact, were under state control. We could think of how to formulate policies that addressed state interests. That era is ending. In fact, that era has ended. Let me tell you what has happened.

At the time of the breakup of the Soviet Union, it had more than 30,000 nuclear weapons. They had more than 15,000 tons of highly enriched uranium and more than 150 tons of separated Plutonium-239. As a scale of comparison—without even getting close to the edge of what you could really do—consider four kilograms of Plutonium-239 and something like 10 kilograms of Uranium-235 as being weapon-significant. That is roughly the size of material in an American baseball. In terms of what you have to smuggle, there is no comparison between that and drugs. I would not recommend that you put it in a condom and swallow it unless you are a health physicist and have a fine understanding of criticality in the human gut. It would certainly give you a new understanding of what a rush means. But it is something that in terms of its physical size is easy to smuggle.

Beyond that, let me say a few things about the former Soviet Union's military inventory. When they were pulled back, they were pulled back very rapidly. There is highly enriched uranium and separated plutonium today in well over—and let me underline—well over 100-plus sites in the territory of Russia alone. Many of the former Soviet nuclear weapons, particularly the small ADMs [Atomic Demolition Munitions], artillery shells, and similar devices, have no, or at best primitive, safety devices on them. They are stored today under poor physical and work conditions with a demoralized guard force and, often, a very demoralized managerial force.

It is not just the former Soviet Union that one has to worry about. The civil sector itself is producing large amounts of plutonium. By the end of the century, there will be well over 1,000 tons of plutonium just in the spent fuel at peaceful nuclear reactors. There will be well over 100 tons of separated fuel. And to shatter another illusion of the last 50 years, in terms of ability to make a weapon, there is no difference between the plutonium that comes out of a peaceful nuclear reactor and that produced in a weapons compound. A weapons designer would prefer to have pure Plutonium-239. You can do it if you have to, and, in fact, we have done it once with civilian plutonium. There are also other weapons complexes around the world—in Pakistan, North Korea, India, China, and South Africa—that still have highly enriched uranium. The supply is there.

Let me look at the issue of buyers and who is interested. It is perfectly true, as Dr. Lee said, we cannot find in Western Europe many cases of North Korea, Iran, Iraq or others buying. Quite frankly, I would be surprised if we did. You know, we have good German policemen on the German border with Poland. We do not have very many good German policemen on the southern routes of the former Soviet Union. There are well developed smuggling routes. There are bastions of criminality in the south, which happens to be closer to Iran and closer to North Korea. There are other ways to get material out rather than coming through Germany. In fact, you would have to be rather stupid, quite frankly, as a smuggler to go through Germany. Some of you know that many of these same southern routes were formerly used by the KGB and others to smuggle western goods and materials into the former Soviet Union.

Second, do not worry, only cops, journalists, and intelligence agents are buyers. Oh, if that were only so. I suspect the warning—to use the phrase used this morning—"the golden time between warning and destruction" in this field is going to be very short. Remember, just like in drugs, you know what you have intercepted. Right now, you do not have the metrics to know what you have not intercepted. That, in many ways, is the most worrying aspect of this matter.

Let me give you some buyers, buyers I think you ought to worry about: first of all, states like Iran, North Korea, and Iraq. Much—almost all, I would argue—U.S. nonproliferation, counterproliferation policy dealing with this has rested on the fact that, fortunately, it takes a state a long time to acquire the material necessary to make a nuclear weapon (if it produces it itself). In the case of North Korea, the first indications–at least in the open literature–of the North Korean nuclear program were identified in the early 1970s. Even with all that lead time, look how difficult we have found it.

Imagine what the difference would be in how you would have to deal with the fact if tomorrow morning we woke up and the Iranians announced they had managed to acquire three ex-Soviet nuclear weapons. We seem to have enough of a hard time dealing with the possibility of one or two nuclear weapons in the hands of the North Koreans. The surprise nature of sudden acquisition without the ability to consider how you're going to deal with it from a defense point of view in the Middle East, for example, is something that would make a mockery of the Middle East peace process and destroy it tomorrow morning.

Third, do not underestimate the ability of criminal gangs to figure out how to make money. Let me give you an example both from the United States and from the UK. In the United States, everyone knows the World Trade Center. In Britain, a far more devastating explosion was carried out by the IRA at Bishop's Gate. If, in either device, there had been simply mixed in radiological, non-weapons grade material, or weapons grade Plutonium-239. You would not be reoccupying the World Trade Center today. Given the ability to decontaminate a site in the middle of a city, plus the prevalence of American lawyers and the litigation that would flow from that, who would dare send a worker back in knowing that 10 years from now a case of cancer could be claimed.

If, in fact, the contamination had been Plutonium-239, the emergency workers who responded to the World Trade Center would not have had detection devices that would detect either the alpha off of 239 or the neutrons. The geiger counters that you see–and that is the standard stock of the New York City Fire Department—would not detect the presence of plutonium. We are so unprepared for that.

Let me say a few things about what I think can be done and really does need to be done. First, we need to recognize that this is a problem. I would like to read you just three statements, all given in a one-week period of August of this year, and see if you can identify who they came from.

"Not a single gram of Plutonium-239 has been missing from storage in Russia."

"The current hullabaloo has a purely economic purpose. The West is trying to foist on us its assistance in the construction of new storage places and installation of their control system. This would mean orders to their firms running into many millions."

"We are not aware of what I would describe as a black market for diverting fissile material. In many cases, the people who are in possession of this diverted material have to go out and find buyers. Thankfully, we're not aware that there are many buyers around and about."

The first two statements are fairly easy. They are from Russia. The third statement, which is not terribly different, if different at all, is from the U.S. State Department. As long as you treat it as if it is not a problem, you are not going to solve it. It has to be raised to the highest level. It is important that it be treated at the summit as a major national security threat. It is a threat to the survival of this country, to the survival of our allies. Indeed, the Russians have to realize, as a government, that it is a threat to their control of their society.

Second, we have to deal with the serious issue that the Russians do not have a clue, in the sense of which we measure our stockpile, of how much material they have. It is one of the dirty little secrets of the cold war that, although many of us had to suffer at international meetings with the Russians—the Soviets in those days—telling us how good their control system was, that it was every bit as good as ours, they did not measure their nuclear material at the physical-limit level. They had a very tight physical control system. It was the KGB. That is in disarray now. The Russians simply do not know how much material they have.

If you do not know how much material you have, how do you know if any of it is missing? And, if you do not know any of it is missing, how, in fact, do you treat the claim: "I have some. If you don't pay off or a political demand is not met, we, in fact, will put it in your water system." There are a lot of other better ways than water systems, by the way, if you want to really be fiendish. In fact, let me say, every American city is surrounded by a far better delivery mechanism than their water system for dispersing radioactive material in a way that would be very difficult to clean up. So we, in fact, have to deal with the issue of control.

Third, we have to put in the hands of the people who are, in fact, on the front lines—the border police and the police—the tools for detecting nuclear materials. It would be hard to realize how primitive those tools are. During a two-year period when I was based in the United Kingdom, I used to periodically get calls, all at odd hours of the morning and the night, from someone reporting that the German Federal Police or the Bavarian Highway Police had just stopped a car and it had a trunk full of Uranium-235, weapons-grade uranium.

Without knowing anything else, I could say "I can tell you one thing. They may have uranium. I doubt that they are really sure of that. But they have not a clue as to what the isotopic composition is. That is not something that you do with a Breathalyzer." Police and border controls around the world are massively unequipped to deal with this problem. Until we give them the equipment and the pay and the encouragement and raise the importance, you are not going to do anything about that.

Fourth—and I will stop here, although there are a number of other steps that could be taken—we as a country have got to come to terms with the fact that one of the legacies of the cold war is the material for nuclear weapons. Uranium, we can figure out how to deal with. We can burn it in reactors, those countries that will still have reactors in 10 years. But we have not made a single move as to how to dispose of our own plutonium. We should not be surprised that the Russians are not rushing to get rid of their plutonium. The safe and assured destruction and disposal of plutonium is one of the highest priorities if, in fact, you hope to control the illegal movement of nuclear materials.

Let me finally give you a clue as to how long you have to do this. The Russians claim they are dismantling 2,000 weapons a year—33,000 weapons. This is a two-to-three decade-long problem. And that is just dismantling the weapons, not disposing of the material. This is not a problem that is going to drop off the agenda tomorrow morning. In fact, if it drops off the agenda this week, one ought to really be concerned. It is a problem that is going to be with us for, I would predict, as long as the cold war took to build up those weapons. And it is going to cost as much to destroy and dismantle the weapons as, unfortunately, it cost to build them.

Question and Answer Session

Mr. de Borchgrave: Dr. Kay, as I understand the total figure allocated by the Nunn-Lugar amendment, it is $1.2 billion to take care of some of the problems you have sketched out so brilliantly. I wonder what your view is as to why we are going to manage to spend only $3 or 4 million on the security and the inventory of all these materials. Is it because the Russians are reluctant to let us know how inadequate the inventory bookkeeping has been or are there other reasons that I do not understand?

Mr. Kay: I think there are two principal reasons. One, in the conditions of Russia today, it is easy to spend money quickly, it is not easy to spend it well. If you want to spend it well, it is going to take time.

Second is that I think the Russians have a great deal of suspicion that, when we talk about material accountancy control, when we talk about safety, that what we want to do is remove their last vestige of superpower status to get into the heart of their nuclear program. It is a legitimate and understandable suspicion, given the period of the cold war. I think, for example, we have made progress in the last few months.

These are steps indicating that we, in fact, are going ahead with our own dismantling program to give them reassurance. It is going to take time because this really does rest on trust.

I think some of us who deal with Russians on a daily basis are coming to understand that they are less a government in the modern twentieth century sense than they are a series of feudal empires. The Ministry of Atomic Energy in Russia is the largest single employer in all of Russia. Having that job, having that empire is a source of wealth and power and security and of survival. Anything that threatens or is viewed by those who control the ministry as threatening their position is something they are going to resist. It is going to take a tremendous political effort at the highest levels of both governments to deal with that insecurity.

Dr. Lee: I would like to make a comment on that. I spent about seven weeks in Russia this summer trying to talk to Russian officials, trying to establish a dialogue with people in the Ministry of Atomic Energy and also in the various Russian law enforcement agencies on this whole question of nuclear trafficking. I had very little luck getting anything out of the Russian officials on this issue. These people take the view that unfortunately the West is trying to interfere in and control their nuclear establishment. That is one side of the story.

The other side, though, is that if you go and actually talk to the people who work in nuclear enterprises themselves, you get a somewhat different picture. At that level, I found that people are much more willing to talk about the dangers of theft, leakage, and proliferation. In some cases, they will go into considerable detail about the specific types of problems of inventory control, accounting, and physical security. So, it really depends, I think, very much on which level you are talking on.

I think it is probably a lot more productive right now to deal with people in the enterprises and installations themselves rather than trying to fight or refight the cold war all over again with senior Russian officials.

Question: Do we have any wherewithal within our emergency management resources and organizations to deal with this, at least within the United States?

Mr. Kay: There is a nuclear emergency capability, NEST [Nuclear Emergency Search Team], for dealing with it in the United States. The problem is, it was predicated on an image of the problem that is not really the most likely problem—the theft of a U.S. nuclear device. You are much more likely now to face either a jerry-rigged nuclear device or a Russian, Soviet-designed device. The Russians have been very wary of sharing with us information on the design of their weapons, even when we explained that we may need the information because we may have to take one and disarm it. That is part of the legacy of the cold war.

The NEST capability needs to be vastly increased. Finding a nuclear weapon today in an urban environment is a nightmare unless you actually have a good source of human intelligence on it. I have said for a long time that, if I had to smuggle a nuclear weapon into the United States, my preferred method would be to put it in a bale of marijuana. I can contract out the delivery. There is a well-developed route structure. I know exactly what my chances of getting through are. And it happens that marijuana is a good shielder of the radiation, the small amount of radiation that comes off a nuclear weapon.

CHAPTER 6

The Crime Without Borders: A British View

David Veness
Assistant Commissioner Metropolitan Police
New Scotland Yard, England

Judge Webster: It is my privilege this afternoon to introduce David Veness, the assistant commissioner of the Metropolitan Police, New Scotland Yard.

You heard Buck Revell earlier talk about the ITLO-American relationships and Canadian cooperation. I want to say that no other country in the world enjoys with us this special relationship that we have with the law enforcement and intelligence agencies of the United Kingdom. Throughout 14 years of my own experience in government, there was never a time when our agencies could not work together, could not solve problems together, and could not do it better because we were working together.

Commissioner Veness joined the Metropolitan Police Cadet Corps in 1964 and ultimately trained as a hostage negotiator in 1979. He became one of England's leading negotiators and taught this rapidly rising art and science, then participated in the Iranian Embassy siege in 1980 and the Libyan People's Bureau incident in 1984, as well as being an adviser and counselor in incidents occurring across Europe, North and South America, and in the Middle East.

He was appointed a commander in 1987 and subsequently became Commander Public Order, Territorial Security and Operational Support. In addition to the conventional duties of that post, he dealt with policing matters in the Gulf War.

In 1991, he was promoted again and took command of the specialist crime squads at Scotland Yard, which include serious, organized, and international crime, the fraud squad, the flying squad, the crime operations branch, criminal intelligence, and force firearms. He is also secretary of the Chief Officers Committee of the South East Regional Crime Squad, which was formed in April 1993. On April 5, 1994, he was promoted to assistant commissioner, "Specialist Operations."

It is a real privilege that we introduce one of the finest in our special relationship, Commissioner Veness.

David Veness

We like to think that the linkages between UK and U.S. law enforcement are undetectable; they are, indeed, seamless. I am happy to stand here and make that statement today. Thank you as well to CSIS for the opportunity to be here and to contribute to this enormously important agenda-setting conference.

My views are not a national United Kingdom perspective but those of a London detective who is privileged to command the squads and branches engaged in special operations at Scotland Yard. (Let me immediately reassure you that the young men and women are much better than their bosses.)

I will seek to suggest to you why we see the need to monitor organized crime, how we do that, and what use we make of that monitoring for operational activity. My message this afternoon could really be summarized briefly: mobility and the interdependence of nations. Because, whilst my views are based in London, it is impossible to address organized crime in the United Kingdom other than in the regional and, for us, the European context. I will endeavor to prove to you that Europe is part of the solution as well as part of the problems we have heard about today.

My thesis is that serious and organized crime is entirely motivated by profit. It follows that unfettered or easier mobility of persons and property will always be exploited by criminals to gain access to profit wherever it may be found. Untraceable, untaxable income in the hands of criminals is the new lingua franca of organized crime. The link between Medellín and Moscow is the $100 bill. The European exchange rate mechanism may not yet work for Britain and the European community, but its Mafia equivalent is extremely effective.

Our responsibility in law enforcement is to spot these financial strands whilst they are emerging threads and not wait until they become chains. It is to be expected that the speed of criminal exploitation, of opportunities created by mobility, will exceed the response of the authorities. There are reasons for this. First, the authorities, all of us, need to shed the mentality of institutions and agencies that have been designed for different purposes.

Second, the authorities need to cross the divide created by our own national interests. If we date the contemporary process of enhanced mobility in Europe to 1989, it is likely that, in 1994, the operations, intelligence, and communications of criminals are better than that of the authorities. And in those nation-states, where the period of upheaval since 1989 has meant a substantial revision of political, social, economic, and legal structures, the criminals will have and, indeed, have made even more significant gains. Put simply, in 1994, throughout greater Europe and Eurasia, the threat of serious crime is more serious than the response.

A simple statement. No law enforcement agency anywhere, acting alone, has ever sustained a successful attack on organized crime. The message is interdependence. If we think that organized crime is capable of local action by any one agency, we merely demonstrate that we do not understand the problem. The ideal is multidisciplinary, multiagency, multinational endeavors, but built on solid local foundations. We are, sadly, very far from that ideal. At a recent conference at which several in this room were represented, this point was made very graphically by the president of Turkey.

If I can turn to the threats for the United Kingdom and address them at three levels: local crime, overseas crime, and, indeed, the combination of local and overseas criminals. In order to do so, it is necessary to distinguish between serious crime and organized crime groups. Serious crime arises from the grave nature of individual offenses or by the collective scale of more minor offenses. Organized crime has distinguishing characteristics, including, among others, accumulation of profit, persistence and longevity, systematic activity (often international), a structured and compartmentalized hierarchy, a propensity to violence, perversion of commerce, political influence, corruption of various agencies, and, always, the availability of lawyers and accountants.

United Kingdom local criminals are professional and extremely effective, but they are not all organized according to this criteria, although some are very close indeed. Within serious crime in the UK, there are no Mr. Bigs, but there are many who are a bloody sight bigger than they ought to be. They operate in networks or cooperatives through which supplies and services can be combined according to need. These networks can span Europe. The main activities of local, serious, UK criminals are drugs, robbery, fraud, forgery, counterfeiting, vehicle theft, and high class burglary.

There are various overseas criminal groups active within the United Kingdom. They represent, primarily, the organized crime influence. The Italian Mafia, in its various forms, is present in the United Kingdom for money laundering, fraud, and drug trafficking. There has been a growth of the spread of Mafia interests throughout France as a result of the success—and very welcome it is—of the Italian authorities.

Some suggest that it is in the Mafia interest to pursue an insidious, low-key policy in the United Kingdom, avoiding gratuitous violence and maximizing profit from its diversified investment. Claire Sterling very correctly has reproved us for our past indifference to Mafia activity within London and the rest of the United Kingdom. I reassure her that is not the position today. Indeed, we see a move beyond money laundering to other more overt forms of criminal activity. And we enjoy an enormously close exchange with our Italian colleagues and are pleased to welcome them permanently in London.

Next on the list of overseas criminals are the Colombian cartels, classically, in contemporary terms, from Cali, actively targeting the whole of Europe, including the United Kingdom, for cocaine trafficking and money laundering. Drugs are being moved through the European bridgehead, through the southern entrance of Spain and Portugal, and increasingly through the turntable ports (as they are described) of the Baltic states and St. Petersburg, an outpost of activity for Poland and Hungary.

The Triad societies, next on the list, display a propensity for extreme violence and are involved in drug dealing, money laundering, fraud, forgery, extortion, and illegal gaming. They operate mainly within the Chinese communities, but also, in modern terms, through the Vietnamese.

Next are the Caribbean criminals, including a triangle that links the United Kingdom, the Caribbean, and the Eastern Seaboard of the United States. Those groups arguably exist on the borderline of the definition of organized crime because of some degree of lack of internal organization. But the activity is formidable. It occurs in cannabis and cocaine trafficking, and the distribution, as in the UK and here, is dangerous because it occurs mainly in our depressed, inner-city areas and is constantly reinforced by the use of firearms. These criminals thus represent not only a criminal problem, but a social and public order threat.

For us, West Africans are active in drug trafficking and fraud, and the scale of the fraud is very significant indeed. Asian subcontinental criminals are engaged in heroin importation and money laundering. Eastern European criminals represent an emerging phenomenon for us, and firm indications already exist of involvement in extortion and smuggling within various European countries.

Some Russian—and I am tasked to include Chechen, Azeri, Georgian, and Ukrainian—criminals strike us as different not only in what they do but the way that they do it. The ruthless use of violence gives us cause for concern. The trafficking in firearms is worrying for an almost unarmed society such as the United Kingdom. We, interestingly, have more to lose than any other Western European nation from the criminal use of firearms because of our predominantly unarmed position.

The present impact of crime from central and eastern European origins within London is money laundering. You would expect that. London is the closest of the three great global financial centers of the world to central and eastern Europe. We are engaged in a wide-scale research program led by our National Criminal Intelligence Service to delve into the scope of the problem. Our fears begin with guns, but also with drugs, primarily from the southern states of the former Soviet Union. The unequivocal advice from our Russian colleagues, with whom we enjoy very close relations, is that we have the money now; we can expect the men, certainly, within two to three years.

If I may build upon the remarks made this morning by the director of the FBI, may I say that we in European law enforcement applaud the FBI's links with Russia and the intent to station officers in Moscow. The U.S. initiative is enormously important in terms of leadership and resources. But, if I may say so from a European perspective, we need to work in partnership and to coordinate with existing European efforts. I know that is recognized. We should not forget that the chiefs of police in Berlin and Warsaw are closer to the problem than most and have a great deal to contribute.

As an example of ongoing cooperation—and it is not to the East, but it is important here—I should cite the joint U.S.-UK initiative in the dependent territories in the Caribbean. This joint task force is staffed by the FBI and Scotland Yard fraud squad officers working under the umbrella of the National Criminal Intelligence Service. I take the point that there is more to be done, but this is not a fig leaf. We should not dismiss the determination of UK law enforcement in conjunction with our American colleagues. But I come back to the point—and it is, perhaps, a point that I will take away from this day in terms of the message for the future—that, unless the United States leads with this particular threat of global organized crime, there is no solution.

If I may revisit Moscow, there are some strands of optimism emerging. If you look at colleagues within the MVD, within the FSK, and, notably, within the procurators offices, it is important to acknowledge that there are men of determination within those bodies. We need to be pragmatic, but we should not dismiss their efforts. Law and order in Russia is far from inevitable, but it looks a little bit more possible this month than it did last month, despite the enormous remaining problems. Again, as Louis Freeh said this morning, we in law enforcement have no option but to support them. We need to confront the corruption risks. We need to be realistic, but we need to work in partnership.

And, last, on my list of UK problems, there are increasing examples of links between local and overseas criminals. This occurs mainly, at the moment, on the base of individual collective business contacts among UK professional criminals and reflects common interests between overseas organized crime and domestic criminal networks. The potential for such broader partnership is inevitably destined to grow, and there are indications that those links have already been made.

Enough, then, of the problem. What of the solution? What is the agenda to counter the threat. There are six items, and I hope you will notice that the last is about law enforcement. First, we need to recognize the problem, at the national and international level, defining the scope of the problem. We need to approach it on a multiagency basis. If you want a case study of where the absence of multiagency responsibility produces almost chaos, Russia is that at the moment. We need to recognize political defenses, nationally and internationally. We need to build upon professional ethics, politics, law, banking, business, and accountancy to identify the predictable weaknesses, vice and gaming.

And, last, we need to build effective law enforcement. Effective law enforcement is built from the bottom up on the basis of local activity, but it needs to be translated to national criminal intelligence providing analysis and research. We are proud of the fledgling National Criminal Intelligence Service in the United Kingdom. We need to enforce that through organized crime groups. We have an organization based in London known as JAG, the Joint Action Group, which is looking at and dealing with emerging organized crime threats. It is a truly multiagency approach. There are 25 agencies signed up for its activities. We need to generate constructive paranoia. Let us transfer some of the fear from the public we serve to the criminal. Let us create frustration. Let us disrupt and prevent. Let us attack profits, but let us also do that in an atmosphere of detection and prosecution. We need to stretch the imagination of law enforcement.

What specific initiatives can be taken immediately? Enhance technical facilities, cross-border surveillance, use of control deliveries, vigorous acid tracing and confiscation, and the use of a parallel financial inquiry every time an organized crime investigation is mounted. In addition, witness protection across borders, penitent offenders, the use of undercover and informant systems, and analytical systems that are truly international.

A regional policy within Europe should build upon Interpol as a repository of good practice; its European organized crime units and drug units are very effective. We should rapidly develop Europol. The policing ideal of Europol is a combined intelligence and operational unit addressing serious crime, with priorities defined by operational strategy. That is elusive politically, and, until there is a common European criminal law, the operational aim will not be achieved. But, now, we have the reality of a European Drugs Unit based in the Hague supported by the various nations of Europe.

We should extend the Schengen concept, or a related information system. The ideal of the European Union was that there will be a hard external shell and a computer information system to redress the loss of internal borders. We have lost the internal borders. We await the hard external shell. We await the computer information system. We should sustain our training exchanges, especially in central and eastern Europe, at the strategic and tactical level and recognize that there is much to be attained by a task force solution in the short term.

An international policy should be based on national endeavor. For example, all 12 of the current European Union nations would claim to have a national criminal intelligence service. In reality, only three or four have, and there is scope for development. We need to converge geographically the various national representative organizations. The French show us the way at their new headquarters at Nanterre, outside Paris. They have the Europol home base; they have the Schengen home base, and their national central bureau for the international criminal police organization, all co-located with their national law enforcement agencies: international cooperation focused in a geographic sense.

And, if I can end with the quote of the governor of Istanbul, "International cooperation has a realistic future."

Question and Answer Session

Mr. de Borchgrave: The commissioner has kindly agreed to take a few questions. Perhaps I could kick it off by asking you what you thought about the remarks that were made this morning about little sandbar nations in the Caribbean whose names cannot even be found in the mail room of the United Nations, which, apparently, have only one bank regulator for hundreds of banks, and hundreds of thousands of companies have registered there doing a lot of illegal business. What is your reaction to that?

Commissioner Veness: My reaction, sir, is that of a humble police officer and a detective, and not that of a politician. It is, of course, a professional frustration to any detective—and I have experienced it firsthand in fraud squad activities—to run into the anonymity and the cloak of respectability behind which criminality lurks.

I made a brief reference to the fact that UK law enforcement takes this seriously. We have the very welcome, and, indeed, the enormous support of the FBI in that Caribbean Task Force. I think there is a great deal to be done and a great deal of progress to be made. But I hope you will understand that is a matter for politicians and not for cops.

Question: With the abolition of borders within Europe, how is it possible for a national police force to deal with European-wide criminality without a European-wide police force and a European-wide criminal justice system? How big a problem is that, and what should be done?

Commissioner Veness: It is an extremely well-aimed question, and the answer is infinitely less easy to propose than the difficulty.

The great drama that was predicted in relation to all of the evils that would flow from the abolition of internal borders is not yet as evident as the fears that prefaced it. But, as I mentioned, the idea was that there would be a trinity. We would achieve effective law enforcement based upon the fact of the hard outer shell and an effective intelligence system. Whereas there had been blanket customs coverage in the past, there would be intelligence-driven, targeted customs coverage. That is the intention.

Sadly, the reality is, of course, that we are looking at a nation of 12, 16, and one has the weakest link. And there are various points around the circumference of Europe where the coverage in terms of border control and customs is powerless. To describe them as part-time is optimistic in the extreme. So, that is an enormous weakness. The additional weakness is the absence of a common information system that allows us to target and to be intelligence-driven. So, those are the twin frustrations from a law enforcement perspective.

What are the grounds for optimism? We already have the effective European Drugs Unit; that has the support of the 12 nations. We do not yet have a convention that gives that a legal entity, but it is being driven. The expectation is that next month a draft will be available, and, thereafter, the Europol concept will flow, which will be a genuine opportunity to fill some of those gaps. But you have highlighted the fear. It is going to be a question of running to catch up.

I wonder whether we would have embarked upon this great adventure in terms of abandoning internal borders had people known that 1989 and 1990 were around the corner, because that has changed the political backdrop dramatically. I think you see that reflected in the attitudes of the governments, particularly of France.

Dr. Kupperman: I just note—unless I missed it—you did not talk about Middle Eastern terrorism and bombings in London.

Commissioner Veness: I am very happy to do so. The reason I did not was that the theme that I was addressing was organized crime. To be meticulous, if I had covered that in detail, I should have referred to the activities of indigenous domestic terrorist organizations, which have in the past—and we hope that may be capable of political resolution—been heavily engaged in extortion activity, which is quasi-organized crime.

The current activities within London—occurring on the 26th and the 27th of July—were bombs directed against the Israeli Embassy and against a cultural center north of London. We have, as yet, no firm indication. There is an intelligence picture. What I do not have is the evidence to support the intelligence picture at the moment. But our view is toward the East.

Certainly, it appears that prudent security needs to vigorously encompass the fact that as long as the Middle Eastern process with its kaleidoscopic mosaic of possibilities and various national interests continues to unfold—and please, God, that it does so—we need to be very, very vigilant indeed in relation to that very real security threat.

It was almost a miracle that we did not sustain loss of life in those two bombs just 12 hours apart. But if you place a massive car bomb within 50 yards of one of London's busiest shopping streets, it is difficult to consider that a political act. You are right. It is crime.

Mr. Revell: David, given the independence of the British Constabulary, is the National Criminal Intelligence Service working well? If so, do you see it as a model for Europol?

Commissioner Veness: Thank you, Buck. There is no alternative but for the National Criminal Intelligence Service to work well. It is in the complete interests of UK law enforcement that that should happen. Indeed, there are enormously promising signs that it is growing into the reality. There will inevitably be emerging difficulties with any fledgling organization. But you are absolutely right. The best use that Europe could make of the next few months and years as Europol emerges is to build from the bottom up. If each one of the European nations had a truly focused National Criminal Intelligence Service, drawing together the energies of all of its disparate operational and intelligence services, then the European picture would be very effective, indeed.

It may be possible to think in terms of a vision, almost a pyramid. If one has at the bottom level the various NCISs of Europe, then that grows to the next level, which is at the regional tier. It is, perhaps, not inconceivable that in a few years we can see that— the pyramid will be global in terms of National Criminal Intelligence Services and that Europol could speak to Asiapol or Americapol.

Question: On what do you base your feeling of optimism about the situation in Russia? Because, statistically at least, since the beginning of this summer, the numbers of contract murders, et cetera, in Russia itself are setting a record. So, why are you optimistic?

Commissioner Veness: That is a very good point and it is optimism with a very little "o," let me stress. What do I base it on? Not much. But I base it on having been there several times and worked closely with colleagues and seen that our operational contexts have now moved at a dramatic pace. Whereas cases that we were working together were very rare, indeed, in 1993—by the end, once a month—there are cases now once a week where there is mutual activity between Scotland Yard and our activities and associates in the MVD.

My optimism, a little "o," is based upon a slight change of mood. I detected a few weeks ago a greater sense of resolution and determination. To what extent that may have been associated with the decrees I am not politically adept enough to judge. But, certainly, among our colleagues in the MVD and the FSK, there seems to be a little bit more of the chin in the air as opposed to the doom and gloom that had so depressed us on recent visits. No more than that, but perhaps we build on straw in this particular regard.

Question: Do you see a need for a connection on an operational and intelligence level between the working levels of the European Union's K-4 Group and the U.S. national law enforcement community? And, if so, what is Scotland Yard doing to promote that?

Commissioner Veness: That is a very real need, and I am glad you identified it. As Buck commented, part of the strength of the Trevi structure—which has been predominantly replaced by the structures we now have subsequent to the Maastricht Treaty, although implementation yet awaits—is that we need to retain those very important bridges to which I have referred. One way of doing that is through the bilateral links that are so strong between our countries. Certainly, Scotland Yard has retained its vigor in ensuring that the links between ourselves and our American operational contacts, and more broadly into Europe, are working extremely effectively indeed.

If I may say so, the FBI hardly needs them because of the links that are so effective with the French, German, Dutch, and, indeed, all the other nations within the EU. But the point is recognized. In due course, once Europol achieves an international political personality, then, of course, the bridges can be developed again in a more formal sense. The sticking point is that Europol does not have a legal personality at this stage and, therefore, is constrained in the formal links that it can develop with other legal personalities. That will pass very rapidly with time.

Mr. de Borchgrave: Can I ask you, Commissioner, when you expect Europol to be fully operational in the investigative sense of that word?

Commissioner Veness: It is likely to await, in terms of formal structure, the ratification of the convention. That could be two to three years hence. Operationally, the European Drugs Unit is already delivering. There are European liaison offices (ELOs) from each of the European nations. They are beginning to contribute effectively, both at the intelligence level and in terms of operations. I am afraid this is a question of the police officers having to run ahead of the politicians in order to make that work. I have confidence that if you put 24 hand-picked cops in the Hague, they will deliver you an effective operational service.

Question: What is it that has caused the relative ineffectiveness of the Serious Fraud Office, and how are you handling very large international financial fraud prosecutions and investigations?

Commissioner Veness: The Serious Fraud Office has had a bad press and has had some difficulty with some major cases. As you know, it is an independent entity, so I should ask the director of the Serious Fraud Office to answer that question.

The interdependence between the respective interests (my own fraud squad, the Crown Prosecution Service, which has the Fraud Investigative Group—they are called FIG arrangements to bring together prosecutors, accountants, and fraud investigators at a very early stage—and the role of the Serious Fraud Office) is being very seriously investigated as we speak. I would envisage a merger for more operational effectiveness of those three functions, and I think with confidence one can see that happening. But I recognize why your perception is as it is.

CHAPTER 7

Containing the New Criminal Nomenklatura

Claire Sterling, Chair
Scholar and Author

Mr. de Borchgrave: President Yeltsin said a few months ago that Russia is now the superpower of crime. He described his own country as the biggest Mafia state in the world, and it spans 11 time zones. Hence, the title of our next panel, "Containing the New Criminal Nomenklatura."

In 1991, according to Russian law enforcement authorities, there were roughly 780 Mafia gangs in the former Soviet Union; today, apparently, there are 5,700, including some 3,000 identified godfathers, or "thieves-in-law" as they are called, and about 100,000 members and 3 million worker bees, who are responsible for roughly 35 percent of the Russian GDP. They have relations with 29 foreign countries, according to testimony we heard on the Hill last May 25th. They also run more than 200 gangs in the United States.

No one has exposed this with more diligence and more clarity than Claire Sterling, who is our next chairperson. She has exposed all of this in her latest book. If you are not familiar with it, rush out and buy *Thieves' World*. She also wrote the famous book *The International Terror Network* back in the 1970s, which was widely pooh-poohed—as some of you may remember–because it documented links between international terrorist movements and Eastern European secret services and, of course, did not fit the conventional détente wisdom of the time. She has now been more than vindicated, beyond the shadow of a legal doubt, by the miles upon miles of files pouring out of the archives of former Communist intelligence services.

Peter Grinenko is arguably the country's foremost authority on the Russian Mafia's connections with organized crime in the United States, having spent 15 years tracking first Soviet and then Russian criminals in a wide variety of law enforcement capacities. He was supervisor of detectives for the Brooklyn, New York, District Attorney's Office and a point man for the Federal Organized Crime Joint Task Force, where he worked closely with the FBI, DEA, INS, Customs, and even the Latvian Police Department. He is now a partner in a mergers and acquisitions firm in Moscow and in a security firm in Latvia. He speaks, obviously, perfect Russian, and he has extensive knowledge of Russian business practices and of how American businessmen have become inadvertently involved with organized crime in the former Soviet Union.

Rounding off the panel is Ronald Murphy, the director of the Advanced Systems Technology Office (ASTO) of the Advanced Research Projects Agency (ARPA). In this capacity, Mr. Murphy is responsible for a number of programs, ranging from counternarcotics and aeronautics to intelligence. Prior to joining ARPA, Mr. Murphy worked as an engineer at Boeing, the U.S. Air Force Flight Dynamics Laboratory, and in the U.S. Navy. Having directed numerous high tech projects—both in the "black" and "white" worlds—we are most fortunate that Mr. Murphy has offered to provide some insights into a few organizational and technological initiatives to help us cope with Russian organized crime.

Claire Sterling

Between my first visit to Russia in the fall of 1991 and my last visit just this last summer, I saw more or less the completion of what had promised to be a frightening process and, indeed, did become one, the criminalization of a society. I do not mean by that to criminalize every individual Russian, because there are still brave souls who try to resist, to keep out of the system that has emerged. But the system that really dominates every aspect of political, economic, and social life in Russia is a criminalized system.

It is very hard to talk about containing the new criminal nomenklatura because that would seem to exclude the political nomenklatura. Actually, I think the serious problem in Russia is that the dividing line between the one and the other is almost invisible—indeed, is invisible. What we are seeing in Russia is a shared monopoly of power between politicians and crooks, and the system works to their mutual advantage.

I want to add to what Commissioner David Veness said about what has happened to international organized crime since 1989 and 1990. What has happened, of course, has been the disappearance of the frontier between East and West—fortunately, for the West, until then very heavily guarded on the eastern side. Since that time, the frontier has not been guarded, essentially, on either side. Although efforts are being made on the western side, they have not yet been successful.

The result of that has been an additional dimension to the whole phenomenon of international organized crime that is almost beyond describing. It is true that, even before the collapse of the Berlin Wall and the falling away of that frontier between East and West, there was a growing tendency of the big transnational organized crime groups to work together, set aside their differences, and take advantage of the economy of scale involved in every form of licit and illicit activity that could make money. But with the emergence of the Russian Mafia, this phenomenon has taken an enormous spurt forward. I will give you what may seem like a modest example of what this means.

A couple of months ago, an Italian organization called the Confederation of Public Exercise Enterprises (which means bars, restaurants, discos, et cetera) issued a report on organized crime, racketeering, and so on. The report covered almost for the first time, in some detail, what had happened with the Sicilian Mafia, the Camorra, and the 'Ndrangheta in their activities outside of Italy. It is now accepted that they have, of course, been operating on an international scale, indeed on a global scale, for many, many years.

But with the emergence of the Russian Mafia phenomenon inside Russia and its moving out to the West, we have had the simultaneous moving of Western organized crime groups into Russia and the former Soviet states starting with the Sicilian Mafia and its organized crime partners inside Italy. The Colombian cocaine cartels were more or less simultaneously involved, but the Sicilian Mafia and its Italian partners have been the prime movers in bringing international organized crime into an operational situation inside Russia.

What the confederation report found a couple of months ago and pointed out for the first time in public was that with the opening up of the borders of Russia and the former Soviet states and the introduction of what is called—laughably, perhaps—the free market economy, the possibilities for commerce, for simple consumer goods for which the Russian population was starved, were immediately obvious to the Camorra, the Mafia, and the 'Ndrangheta, but especially the Camorra and the Mafia.

So, they worked out a deal with the Russian Mafia whereby they opened factories in southern Italy to manufacture jeans, fake watches, all kinds of consumer goods, fake Valentino models—every kind of consumer good that Russians had been starved for. They are now producing these consumer goods in vast quantity, and they have the Russian Mafia as their distributor inside Russia. This is a multibillion dollar enterprise that is totally protected, from beginning to end.

The factories that have emerged are giving employment to the unemployed in the south of Italy, which means that a good deal of political cover is now available despite the effort to fight organized crime inside Italy. (It is very difficult to fight any creation of new jobs in southern Italy, in Naples, in the south.) And, of course, the distribution of Western consumer goods, Western jeans, Western shoes, Western shirts, Western fake Valentinos and Armanis is a source of great pleasure to Russian consumers. I have seen some of the fake models selling for $800 in the lobby of the Radisson Hotel, among, probably, some real models as well. It is a small example, but a practical one, of the possibilities that have opened with the emergence of this incredible new organization on the international scene.

The other part of what has happened is that the Russian Mafia organizations have moved very quickly into the rest of Western Europe and into the United States, as we all know. What we, perhaps, are not fully aware of is that in their moving first across the border into West Berlin from East Berlin and from there spreading through Belgium, Holland, Britain, Italy, and especially all through Germany, they have used a triangular arrangement (using the same forces, the same front company, the same export/import companies for their own traffic) between Berlin, the western coast of the European Continent, and the United States. The same people, the same personnel, the same front company now operate from Moscow and St. Petersburg through the East European states, through Germany, through Western Europe, through New York, Miami, San Francisco, and Los Angeles.

It is commonplace to say that this is the biggest multinational or the fastest growing multinational organization in the world. But the part of it that is truly alarming, I think, is not just that it is big and fast growing, but that it is truly multinational in that we now have the sharing of intelligence information, the sharing of resources, the sharing of channels for money laundering on a scale such as we have never seen before.

Those of you who have seen my book perhaps have taken note of the fact that money laundering today has become, in many ways, more profitable than drug trafficking itself. That is, the plebes can do the actual handling of the drug. But the Sicilian Mafia, which has now been entrusted with a good deal of the money laundering on behalf of the Colombian cocaine cartels as well as for its own activities, can get in Russia and Eastern Europe—but especially in Russia—a 25 percent cut from the Colombian cocaine cartels for the money the Mafia is laundering on their behalf. On top of which, it can invest that money in Russian commodities for export for hard currency, which comes out of clean currency at a profit of 200, 300, 400, 500 percent.

This is probably the best washing machine for dirty money that has ever been devised and it is growing apace. It is now perhaps the fastest growing money laundering center in the world. Billions of dollars are now coming into Russia from all over the world for this purpose, because the opportunities are almost unlimited. In the same way, $22 billion a year are going out of Russia. That is, it is not just the foreign criminal money coming in that is being laundered and leaving, but it is the Russian criminal money that is being made by payoff, blackmail, extortion, theft, and especially swindles (bank swindles, white collar crime) that is leaving the country.

Here, I would just like to add a very important reminder to people who may tend to accept a commonly proposed—I am looking for a polite word—"excuse" for the emergence of the Russian Mafia with the kind of power it has. The excuse is, or the soporific explanation is that all capitalist societies begin with brigands and crooks, who, upon making their money, acquire a set of ethics to go with their new position in society. The richer they get, the cleaner they look. Therefore, we have only to expect that upon insisting on thrusting a fast transition to a free market economy on Russia, we are bound to get a bunch of brigands and crooks, the only people with cash possibilities of moving in on the economy. And, indeed, that is what we have gotten.

What this theory fails to point out is that Russian organized crime produces nothing, invests nothing, and is not interested in developing any form of production or any means of furthering the economic welfare of the country. As soon as it makes money, it sends the money out of the country to us, or to Switzerland, or to Austria, or to the Pacific Rim—wherever it is possible to roll their money up into more money. It sends the children here to go to Harvard if they can make it, or to London to go to Oxford and Cambridge. This organization is interested not in any way in building a future for itself inside Russia, but is simply accumulating the most capital possible for its own purposes.

What is happening as a result is that this country (which occupies a sixth of the earth's land mass and 11 time zones—as Arnaud has pointed out) is being systematically plundered, ransacked by a criminal class working directly in hand with the political forces running the country, to the total detriment of the society it exploits. The great majority of Russians get no benefit from this operation. The new class of millionaires constitutes, for me personally, the most nauseating, distressing example of vicious, ferocious, savage imitation capitalism that I have come across.

I believe that this problem has to be addressed not just as a threat to the United States because of the smuggling of nuclear materials—although the nuclear materials are certainly a threat. It is a threat, I think, to American society and to Western society that such an enormous country, such a chaotic and enormous country, is in such a state in which anything can explode. And an explosion of any social kind in that country cannot fail to create catastrophe for the rest of the world. I think, therefore, I would like to offer a modest note of criticism, perhaps, to what the American position has been when the FBI went over and opened an office in Moscow.

The emphasis of opening that office was that "Russia is now a threat to our security. The seepage, the leakage of nuclear materials, is now becoming an immediate problem for our society." Yes, that is true. But I think we should have said at the same time, "We feel an enormous sympathy and concern for the people of Russia, apart from the threat to ourselves, because of what is happening to their own society and what this can mean for them as well as for the rest of the world."

Just a word on the nuclear traffic problem. To my knowledge, trafficking has been going on since 1991 in at least a small degree with uranium, plutonium, and cesium (and any number of radioactive materials—not necessarily all of them usable for the making of nuclear warheads, but all of them extremely dangerous as contaminating radioactive materials). This fact has been known, at least to the authorities of certain countries in Europe. I do not know how many, but, since there are four judges currently involved in Italy alone in handling investigations involving traffickers who have been caught with these materials, it is clear that the traffic has been going on at least that long.

It is furthermore clear, from the first arrests that were made in Italy in the fall of 1991 involving three traffickers who were carrying small quantities of uranium and plutonium, that a network existed in Vienna headed by an ex-KGB colonel called Alexander Kusan, that this network had a vast assortment of crooks, criminals, ordinary traffickers, and businessmen, working for it—several hundred at least—all over Europe, that it was working together with the Sicilian Mafia and the Camorra, and that it was using Vienna as its base of operations, as headquarters, but was also operating heavily on the whole corridor of the Adriatic from Trieste to the borders of Slovenia and into Croatia.

This network has been described in detail by traffickers who were arrested in these first arrests in Como, Italy, in 1991. The texts of their interrogations have revealed the degree to which this network has been supported directly by high officials of the Russian armed forces and by high officials of the former KGB. The traffickers themselves have described their dealings and transactions involving some 20 countries, not all of them necessarily small Third World countries.

I am sorry to say that I cannot agree with the idea that only journalists and undercover sting operators are involved or are largely involved in these operations. It is clear from the evidence gathered by at least the four judges in Italy who are handling these investigations that the traffic is real, that the buyers are out there, and that the dimensions of the traffic are now growing very rapidly.

Ms. Sterling: I will turn the podium over to Peter, whom I know will not agree with me about a great deal of what I have said about the Mafia.

Peter Grinenko

My experience is in dealing with the Soviet criminals, and I like to refer to them as Soviet criminals because that is all they are. They are criminals; this "Mafia" title that they has been given to them by the media, if you go to Russia and you ask somebody, "Where's the Mafia?" they will start by telling you that pre-1991 they are talking about government members.

In Russia, you have a whole different society. We are all the same people, but the mentality is completely different. You have 70 years of communism; it definitely warped the way people think there. In normal conversations with Russians, they will lie to you for no reason, no reason at all. But they want to see if you will catch on. It is like a little test. It is a game. The same thing goes on with what they discuss with you. If they know you are a journalist, they will tell you everything that a journalist is interested in.

My first experience dealing with Soviet criminals was in 1981. It involved the counterfeiting of Russian drivers' licenses. It sounds like Russian drivers' licenses in New York? Yes. They did not want to go through the hassle of getting a New York driver's license. There is reciprocity. So, you come in with a Russian driver's license, and you exchange it. You take a little written test in Russian, and you now have a New York driver's license.

The problem is that most of these people, somewhere in the vicinity of 2,800 at that point, never sat behind the wheel of a car. They would be driving busses and minivans and ambulances, never, never having experienced driving. Try to explain that to the Department of Motor Vehicles or the Taxi and Limousine Commission. "No, that can't be. You're wrong." That is the truth. That was the first case.

As mentioned to you before, counterfeiting—they are great at it. They are fantastic at it. When I was assigned to the Joint Organized Crime Task Force, we had a case involving checks. I will not mention the bank. But the bank cashed $3 million worth of checks that this Russian group made before they realized they were counterfeit. When we turned to the person and we questioned him about how it was done, we were expecting some kind of great revelation. He said, "I walked into that place on Hudson Street and I got the paper. We went to this printer on Mulberry Street, and I got it printed." He did it right up the street. They are excellent counterfeiters.

There are a couple of comments I wanted to make on what Claire was saying. The problem is immense. I have been going back and forth to the Soviet Union since 1987. From 1981 to 1989, I worked in the Joint Organized Crime Task Force. My reputation stemmed from the fact that I locked all of them up and sent them to jail and I had the ability to turn informants, Russian informants.

Early on, there was a homicide of a gentleman by the name of Huey Bruckin. I read about him in *New York Magazine*. He was a dissident. He was a respected author and bright gentleman. Ultimately, as we went into the homicide, we found out he was a scam artist. He used to scam people with diamonds. That was his main act. At that time, I started thinking there is something wrong with this whole situation. I am of Russian descent, but I was born in Germany and I grew up in Bedford-Stuyvesant, New York.

I did a symposium at Fordham University and there was a reporter there by the name of Jerry Capicci. He was very intense about the FBI and law enforcement being ethical and admitting to their problems. When I had my opportunity, I mentioned to Jerry that journalists in the matter involving Soviet criminals create "godfathers." But they are criminals. The problems that we have here in the United States mean they will defraud every government agency that exists starting with Pell Grants to Medicaid to you name it, anything. There are cases galore at the moment.

Furthermore, they are not organized; they are individuals. They are fluid—at most, groups. Occasionally, they will tap on each other to perform a scam or a crime. But beyond that, they are not organized. They do not answer to anybody in particular. They do not have any kind of structure such as the traditional Italian Mafia. The only other good part about it is that I have not met or locked up a Russian in my entire career that would want his children to be criminals, which is one of the things about which I agree with Claire.

Ms. Sterling: They want to send their kids to Harvard.

Mr. Grinenko: That is right. That is what they want. Now, then, let us go across the ocean to Russia. In 1987, when I first started going there, I helped organize some joint ventures. Eventually, one of the joint ventures I organized was the production of Peters cigarettes. But nobody knew me there as being in law enforcement. So, I had this opportunity to be exposed to the Russians as someone wanting to make money there, and I found the level of corruption unbelievable. Corruption is the norm in the former Soviet Union and all its republics. That is the norm. And, in some republics, it is worse than in Russia. Start with Yeltsin on down. Remember, he was a Communist before he became a democrat, and so were the rest of them. They reregistered as democrats. There is something wrong there. Now, from the time that they are able to read, they have been taught that Westerners are dopes. I do not care who you deal with, that person at some point or another was taught that Westerners are dopes. Then, when Westerners come to Russia and are spending dollars all over the place, that Russian looks at him like a dope.

But, let us get back to the level of corruption. Peter the Great imported culture, he did not import ethics. That is the problem. The problem is that general mentality. Each time I go (I am on trip number 47 now—I think) I first ask myself, "Why am I doing this?" I had the greatest job in the world for 22 years, and this was my attempt to prolong that. I was personally extorted there by the top members of police agencies when I was producing cigarettes. That was both in Latvia and in the Ukraine. When we were discussing getting information in law enforcement (going there from the Brooklyn District Attorney's Office), their main concern was, how much are you going to pay us for this information? Not quite the reaction you are looking for.

Try to understand that what you think you see going on in the Soviet Union is not real. It is hard to understand this part, but try to remember. I am sure some of you have read about the Potemkin villages. When the Czarina wanted to travel and her entourage did not want her to see the depth of the poor, they would set up these towns, facades, where everything was fine. Well, they are great at it. I have asked Russians, what is this need to lie? They do not refer to it as lying. They refer to it in 50 different ways, one of the most common being a Russian term that means "hanging noodles on your ears." But, in essence, they will do it.

One of the major problems that exists in the former Soviet Union at the moment is that there is absolutely no support for law enforcement. The people do not trust law enforcement. For it to improve will take decades. There is no trust, and the corruption is unbelievable. My only suggestion to people who are in law enforcement is that when you go there, do not go there with a host in law enforcement; go there with someone else to see what really goes on.

Ms. Sterling: Before I go on to introduce Ronald Murphy, I would just add for the record one paragraph to set the record straight about the existence of an organization, Peter. Forgive me, but this is from the deputy director of the Organized Crime Section 6 Department of the Interior Ministry of Russia, who last spring at a conference in Rome said that "around 40 percent of Mafia gangs use 1,500 front companies for laundering. They control over 40,000 businesses, including 2,000 state enterprises, 4,000 associations, 9,000 cooperatives, 7,000 small enterprises, 407 banks, 47 exchanges for commodities and currencies, and 697 markets."

Whether it's organized or not, Peter, it is pretty big stuff.

Mr. Grinenko: I am not talking about Russia when I talk about "organized." By the way, it is not organized crime, it is gangs over there, a gang structure. You should ask the guy what is he doing about this problem. But it is gangs. It is not Mafia. There is no structure. There is no godfather and all the other stuff that goes on with Italians. And here it is even less structured. It is criminals. That is all they are, and you lock them up like everybody else.

Ms. Sterling: More power to you, Peter.

Ronald Murphy

I am not here to talk about organized crime. What I am here to do today, though, is talk about the ongoing relationships between the law enforcement agencies and the Department of Defense. It has been touched upon here a little bit throughout the day, and I guess I am kind of surprised it has not been touched upon further, given my past association with law enforcement agencies. Is this a technology problem or is this not a technology problem? I do not know the answer to that, of course, but I will explore some of the issues associated with that.

As it says in the program agenda, I am from ARPA. What is an ARPA and why am I here? ARPA is the Advanced Research Projects Agency, and it is, in fact, the central arm of the Department of Defense, and we work for the secretary of defense. It was created in 1958 in response to the Sputnik launch. We got a big surprise during that particular launch, and ARPA was created to look at those very high-payoff, high-risk kinds of areas so that we could give the surprise to the other guys in the future. From that, ARPA represents an arm of change within the Department of Defense. People kind of love us or hate us, but we are there to bring about change: change in the way we do business, change in the way we do things. We have about 120 program managers, mostly civilians with about 25 percent military. We execute an R&D budget of about $2.5 billion a year.

Our scope of activities ranges from research to exploratory development to advanced development, in other words, from making chips to making airplanes and submarines and so on. Some products to note—although there are many of them: About 20 years ago we had a very classified program called "Have Blue," which was a prototype aircraft that was literally the birth of Stealth; it became the F-117 Stealth fighter as you know it today. We developed the mini-GPS receiver (the "Virginia Slims in a pack," if you will), and almost all of our lives are touched by that industry and that technology today. If you have a mouse on your computer, it has its roots in ARPA. If you have heard of something called the Internet, well, before it was the Internet, it was the ARPANET. So, those kind of things come from ARPA. As I say, we are looked at to bring about some revolutionary changes, not evolutionary changes, in what we do.

Now, our association with the law enforcement agencies, while small, has been a relatively solid relationship. Most of it across the board has dealt with information technology. For the last 10 years (I was going to say mostly with the FBI, but, really, it is a variety of agencies), we have had a diversity of products and a diversity of customers. We also have a counterdrug program that is ongoing with them. That is a DOD program, and we execute the R&D part of that for DOD. It deals with surveillance assets, with nonintrusive inspection at border sites, and with what I allude to as the "little James Bond section," which is the "help the operations guy out in the field" area. I am not sure there is any law enforcement agency we have not dealt with in that respect.

The disintegration of the former Soviet Union was a major milestone that has brought our organizations a little bit closer together. Our missions right now look more diffuse—more diffuse threats, regional conflicts, new missions utilizing joint and multilingual coalitional forces. We have to have very rapid response. We have very few exercises to practice those responses. It is a new way of doing business for us. We have to do this with fewer people, with fewer systems, both legacy and new systems, and, now, literally, affordability is the cornerstone—not performance. And I have to tell you that is a key change at ARPA because we would have sold our first child to get a count of drag or a pound of weight off an airplane, but not anymore. We are addressing things a lot differently at ARPA and within the Department of Defense relative to affordability. Affordability reigns supreme.

Our response to this new environment has been to emphasize a mission area that has been around for a long time but has not had a lot of emphasis. This is something we have referred to as "Operations Other Than War." (I will refer to it here as OOTW. I am not going to try to pronounce that because every time I do, I get myself into trouble.) It is really peacemaking, peacekeeping, humanitarian relief, those kinds of things. I like to think of it and characterize it by following. Think of somebody in a foreign country or, maybe, actually, the cop on the beat. He is in a peacemaking, peacekeeping situation. All of a sudden, he finds himself in a very heavy duty fire fight. He wants minimal collateral damage, and yet, right after that, he wants to turn around and be the peacemaker again. We train real well within the military to do combat; we do not train too well in this peacekeeping role. So, a lot of the energies of ARPA and the DOD will be focused on this area.

We have a lot of initiatives going on in the area of affordability, but basically I would emphasize that we are trying to get into commercial products more so than we ever did before, commercial technologies, and to open up to a commercial market base to try to help us out there. In this particular case, that is an important thing to understand.

Recently, Dr. Anita Jones, the deputy director of Research and Engineering for the Department of Defense stated, "There's a significant commonality between the advanced technology needed for OOTW and law enforcement requirements. This creates the opportunity for a win/win partnership for DOD and law enforcement. New technology developed by ARPA for military OOTW can be applied to law enforcement, and this will increase production runs of the products, lowering their acquisition costs for both DOD and law enforcement."

This philosophy has manifested itself in the creation of a Memorandum of Understanding between the Department of Justice and the Department of Defense. That has created a joint program office that is headed by ARPA with a Department of Justice deputy. There are program managers in that office that will be at ARPA. There are program managers from both organizations in this. It is jointly funded. DOD funds will address DOD requirements, and Department of Justice funds will address modifications, spinoffs to that technology that more closely align themselves to the law enforcement agency needs and, we hope, help the transition of those to the law enforcement agencies.

The foundation of this agreement is, of course, that DOD products will be almost identical to Department of Justice products. Although the technological underpinnings are essentially identical, there are other differences that present significant challenges, I believe, for both of our organizations to meet these goals. I break these challenges into three areas.

The first is that there are some 17,000 local, state, and federal law enforcement organizations. As I view it, each of them have independent requirements, independent purchasing power, and purchasing decisions. How can we bring these together to better understand the requirements and bring about a unified buying position from them? That is the first thing. Because, if it remains as diffuse as it is right now, it would be very, very difficult to address what are the real requirements.

Second, even with consolidation of this market, it is not clear that many of these needs can be met with an affordable product. We are working very hard to try to address that issue.

The third area, which I think is very important—and I am learning more and more about this every day—is the broad area of consideration relating to the development of products for the law enforcement community that maintain the highest standards of civil liberties and rules of law. The chain of evidence is not particularly a consideration in DOD products, but it certainly is within the law enforcement agencies. Liability and lawsuits, they are not drivers within the development of products we do, but they certainly are with you folks.

Finally, the concepts of operation and the actual rules of engagement, the implementation of these products in the end, is much, much different between our two organizations. I have gone from to talking to technologists and to the operators, or users–if you will—to talking now to the lawyers more than I am talking to anybody else, mostly because of these liability issues in this whole area that I put under the guise of chain of evidence. If we are to have a successful program, we must learn how to deal effectively with these differences not at a technological level but at a real operational level and let that, then, float back to the technology and see if you need new technology or not. As I said earlier, today's seminar is really the first chance I have had to better understand global organized crime, and it has been a real eye-opener.

Given the national security strategy of engagement and enlargement, which requires DOD to place emphasis on nonproliferation, counterproliferation, and counterterrorism, it certainly would seem to me that, in the future, there is potentially a lot of overlap between the missions and requirements for both of these organizations. I guess what I am telling you now is there seems to be a mechanism in place that, if you feel you need technology, you can introduce it through this particular Memorandum of Understanding. We can take a look at it and wring it out and see where we go from there.

In closing, I would like to offer for your consideration some of these following comments. I guess these come about from spending two or three years trying to work some very difficult, complex problems within the Department of Defense, working jointly within the military services. All those services are highly stovepiped, and it is not an easy thing to get them to work together.

I would like to say, while there will always be technologies and gadgets that will allow us to do our job in a more effective fashion, I would encourage you not to focus on this area alone. I do not say do not focus on it, but do not focus on that area alone. This kind of bottoms-up investment strategy, while it may appear successful on the surface, will not in my estimation provide the real strategic results that you all desire.

You can go out to every person who has something to do with your area, and he will always say something like, "If I had this, it would make my life a lot easier." I am sure each one of those products would, in fact, make his life a lot easier. Let us say we were wildly successful because, obviously, we will only be able to do a few of those. Let us say we were wildly successful with making all those work. My estimation in the end is that you have just helped a bunch of folks across the spectrum, but you have not contributed significantly to the overall strategy.

What you must come up with are methods and techniques and models and some kind of capability that will allow you to study the problem from a strategic level down. As you go through this analysis, you must open up the solution space. That is a term I use quite regularly. I guess the analogy within the Department of Defense would be the following. We stack all kinds of regulations on people. We stack all kinds of requirements. Then we tell them how much to build it for. Then we give them a solution space that is about this big. And we have some difficulty in making those work sometimes.

What I am telling you is that our approach has been to open up that solution space in as many dimensions as we possibly can. If that means ignoring traditional organizations and roles and missions and the way we do business today, then so be it. You need to define your high-leverage areas and focus those investment strategies on them. You do not want to say "Gee, in 25 years, we will have a good analysis of this. Then we will just tell you what we need to do."

So, somewhere between those things, you have got to have a balance. Somebody mentioned earlier, I think David Kay, that this is a real difficult problem because you do not really have a baseline here. If you have a baseline of understanding of where you are going, then you have a hope of getting an analysis that might help you understand where you want to go in the future. But you really do not have—at least as I listen to everybody today— it does not appear to me that you have a real solid baseline from whence to move.

Within DOD, the last few years have shown that information technology and the associated command/ and control is one of the highest leverage items that we have. I believe in order to really do more with less, which is certainly what we are trying to do, and to get inside those enemy timelines, if you will (a bit of military jargon, but that is really what you are trying to do also), my feeling is that you really will need superb situational awareness while, as we talked earlier, denying the enemy situational awareness on you. You are going to have to share heterogeneous databases and have expert database navigators that intelligently negotiate these networks that everybody sort of talks about here, and you have to display it in a friendly fashion such that somebody can understand it and you do not have to be a Ph.D. to figure out what is going on.

We will need multiple intelligence correlation capability to correlate all information on a specific target. And I think, what is maybe more important, we will need collaborative planning capability to take advantage of the expertise and the knowledge of every agency. You will require, I believe, the latest in simulation capabilities to aid in understanding the evolving strategies, training, and operation.

Accomplishing this will take not only innovation in technology, but innovation in your concepts of operation, your command and control architectures, your organizational structures. I think your legal constraints have to be opened up and be looked at. Certainly, the rules of engagement, as I believe you mentioned earlier, may have to change somehow to address some of these.

Last but least, my personal hang-up with a lot of this teaming is that we now award people for their individual merits. That drives us into situations where they do not want to share information because information is, in fact, king. "If I have that information, I can, in fact, do my job better than you can do your job, and I will get rewarded for it." I think at the basis of all of this is a system of awards and rewards that are given to organizations and to individuals that somehow accommodate this new way of doing business. I think you have to look at all those dimensions in order to solve the problem that you have here.

I cannot tell you if you need technology or not. But I certainly would not enter into this thinking that you do need technology. You need to enter into this trying to understand what are your problems and where do you need help. If, in fact, technology is the solution to that, then you do, in fact, need technology. If it is not, then you certainly do not. All I would say in closing is that we do, as I said earlier, have a mechanism now where we can effectively deal with studies, as this ongoing study will be, and we will certainly—to the best of ARPA's ability—contribute to that study if we are asked. You will have a way to possibly get to ARPA and the Department of Defense to help out if you do need some work done in those areas.

Question and Answer Session

Mr. de Borchgrave: Before we get into questions, I just wanted to point out that last Monday, I was with the German intelligence community, on Tuesday with the French intelligence community. Everyone, to the last man and woman, agrees with Claire that this is thoroughly organized. They have been followed back and forth—Russian godfathers showing up in Los Angeles, going back to Moscow. There is a direct link, and they have forged alliances with American organized crime. They had a summit meeting on a yacht chartered in Monte Carlo last July, and they cruised off the French Coast—the Russians, even people from Hong Kong, Americans. Every intelligence agency knows about this.

Jonas Bernstein has his hand up. He is based in Moscow and reports for the Washington Times and writes for the *American Spectator*. I think I got that right. Jonas, did you have something?

Mr. Bernstein: Yes, I just wanted to make a comment, and then actually ask a question.

First of all, my question of organized versus unorganized. I think, in a way, both of you are right because you have many corrupt and organized crime gangs. You can argue about their level of organization versus the Cosa Nostra. But to me, the salient feature is the integration with official corruption.

Essentially, you could look at the whole country as a Mafia in this sense. But, if you just look at the individual organized crime gangs, that is not sufficient to tell you what is going on. It is completely, seamlessly, involved with official corruption and that is, I think . . .

Mr. Grinenko: That is right. You are absolutely correct.

Mr. Bernstein: I will give you an example, and this leads up to a question.

Earlier this summer *Rossiskaia Gazeta* ran an article. It claimed that Washington has a list of Russian citizens with U.S. bank accounts into which narcotics money has been deposited and that this list includes top Russian officials. (The word—I do not remember the word in Russian, but it was "top.") Now, I do not know if this is true, but one does hear this sort of rumor very much around Moscow. The Russians I know who follow this question very closely are convinced that the system is rotten from the head down.

So, the question is, if that is the case, from a political point of view, an American foreign policy point of view, is not our close embrace of the Yeltsin administration really inevitably going to work at cross purposes with the anti-Mafia struggle?

Ms. Sterling: If you are asking me that question, the answer is yes. In fact, I would like to go a little further than that. I think that Western authorities generally, and the

United States very much in particular, bear a very grave responsibility for the extraordinary exponential growth of organized crime in Russia and its spread outside of Russia by the extraordinary shortsightedness and lack of attention that has been paid to this problem.

As far as I can tell, no priority was given to this problem by any arm of the American government, whether it be State or intelligence or any other agencies in a position to watch. I do not believe that any other Western country really looked carefully at this problem or reported it even to its people back home until very recently. The only country possibly to be excepted is Germany, because Germany was the first frontline state to be invaded by the new Russian Mafia forces.

But, certainly, the State Department and the White House, the Washington establishment's insistence upon only supporting one man—that is a different kind of political question. But refusing to confront this man with the very obvious evidence of what was going on within his government, among his own cabinet ministers, in light of the facts that have been established by the Russian Parliament, itself, apart from any newspaper reports or anything else that has come from abroad, it seems to me a criminal lack of attention has been paid for which we will all be paying heavily, I am sorry to say.

Mr. Grinenko: Can I comment on that a little bit? About two years ago, a gentleman, also in law enforcement, said to me, "You know, Peter. Yes, you have locked them up. You had investigations. You have got the running record on how many Russians you put in jail and how many of them are dead as a result of identifying them as criminals." But I read a lot. Now, this gentleman talks about reading something in a Russian paper that I believe less than American papers. You mentioned people from other agencies in France and Germany, and I have my own opinion of that.

Mr. de Borchgrave: Plus the FBI and the CIA.

Mr. Grinenko: That is fine. Okay. Obviously their sources are much better than mine, and they probably have many more arrests and have had much more exposure to these Russians than I had.

I do not see in the United States an organized Russian Mafia. I see in Russia a very structured gang system and–absolutely correct—well integrated into the government. The difference is pre-coup and after-coup. Pre-coup, the government kind of ran the criminals. After-coup, the criminals are kind of running the government.

Ms. Sterling: One hundred percent agreed.

Mr. Grinenko: Well, there we go. It is gangs, and you treat them as gangs. Five months ago I was in Russia. There was a gentleman, a Georgian, recently killed. He was standing out by his car, and he got shot. The rumor was that the police did it. His friends did it. His wife did it. It will never be investigated. It will never be solved.

I was there. I just came back three days ago. Last week, a bomb went off. A guy got blown up. I knew him. He was a criminal, okay? A gang leader. They are always concerned about getting blown up. He told me that, and he was. His fears were well taken.

The other problem is, are they coming here? Yes. Criminals are going to come here. But they are coming here because it is too dangerous for them to be there.

Ms. Sterling: No. They make a lot of money here.

Mr. Grinenko: I will quote you a guy. He says, "I just want to come to New York and live a normal life now. I can't stand watching over my shoulder because of these young guys coming up." Now, do the French tell you that?

I am sorry. I do not mean to be argumentative. My problem is that I had experience with the BKA. I hope I am not insulting anybody. But in 1985, I made an arrest involving some Russians. Inadvertently, it led to getting a guy in Berlin, and we brought him back to the United States. Then we developed a relationship with the BKA, and three years later the BKA visited us bringing all their information. (I was out of the FBI Task Force at that time and for three years I had been sending the BKA all sorts of photos and information. That is communicating, okay.) Three years after I started communicating with them, we met, drank a little, talked, and laughed. The next day we got together to review all their information. There was not one tidbit of information there that I did not give them. Not one photo, not one name.

Ms. Sterling: But that was ...

Mr. Grinenko: Germany. Now, France ...

Ms. Sterling: If I might add, that was 1991, Peter. By now ... I mean, let us be fair. By now, the BKA is far ahead of any Western entity.

Mr. Grinenko: I disagree with that 1,000 percent.

Ms. Sterling: ... including the FBI. Sorry, the BKA ...

Mr. Grinenko: You are listening to the wrong Russians, trust me.

Ms. Sterling: No, no. I am not listening to the Russians here, Peter.

Mr. Grinenko: You are listening to the wrong Russians.

Ms. Sterling: I have watched the BKA catch on to what was being done to their country by Russian organized crime and set up special forces to watch the phenomenon as no other law enforcement agency in the West has watched it up until now.

Mr. Grinenko: Please.

Ms. Sterling: They are far more closely involved in the back-and-forth movement between Germany, Moscow, St. Petersburg. They know the names. They know the divisions. They know the front organizations. They know what groups are operating from Berlin to Antwerp, to Miami, to Los Angeles, to San Francisco, to New York, and that is a lot more than anybody else knows.

Mr. Grinenko: Well, they did not know that someone I know was going to get blown up.

Ms. Sterling: That is not their department.

Question: One of the things that Claire had talked about and one of the themes was organized crime and the opportunity to transport fissionable materials to some sort of "Doctor No" someplace who may then threaten the free world and hold us all hostage. One of the things I was interested in that Ron Murphy talked about is that you have to look at what your problem is and then decide whether technology fits or not.

What I wanted to ask Ron is that I think that Congress has put some money aside to try to solve this problem with the passage of the Nunn-Lugar amendment. Regarding the leakage of fissionable materials or production-grade plutonium that might be going across the borders despite the Nunn-Lugar amendment, I wonder if you could take a second and just try to sort of gloss over the top of that for us.

Mr. Murphy: Yes, I would gloss over the top of it since, to my knowledge, appropriations is not done yet. But my understanding is that there may be some money set aside to do some things in this area. I guess I am not exactly sure what will come out of the bill so, again, I do not really want to comment on that.

Question: My question is just about whether technology has a basis of working in this problem kind of area?

Mr. Murphy: Well, I think so. We are working this fairly heavy duty. I mean, the Nunn-Lugar stuff does not come through ARPA, it all comes through the Atomic Energy folks in DOD, Harold Smith. They are putting together a whole program to address that. ARPA has proposed to them multiple programs, many addressing the specific issues you are talking about. We make a bit of a living out of microminiaturization of things, and I cannot go into that any further than having said that. But, we have an understanding that that is a problem, and we have some potential solutions to it.

In the past when we have worked with the law enforcement folks, we went to their R&D people and we collectively produced this thing that we thought was God's gift to whatever we were trying to accomplish. And by God, it worked. Well, it did cost a billion dollars and, you know, you could not carry it around with you and so on and so forth. We avoided looking at the real operational implications and, again, the rules of engagement and so on. In the future, we are not going to do that. We need to get directly to people. We need to look at it more as a system. My concern about some of the congressional issues is—I will be very careful how I word this statement—there certainly is no systems understanding from Congress. They are putting various things in to do, and we will, of course, if it is in the law, do this. It bothers me somewhat that this is the process that is being used. Hopefully, again, this new organization that we are talking about under this Memorandum of Understanding will sort some of that out. Beyond that, I guess I feel a little uneasy talking about the specifics of things.

Mr. Grinenko: I would just like to make a quick comment. I am sorry. Regarding the situation with the fissionable material coming out of the Soviet Union, do not be concerned about organized crime or criminals. The gentleman is absolutely right, okay? Organized crime or gangs or whatever you want to call it, criminals in Russia are making too much money controlling kielbasa there. They are not concerned about fissionable materials, okay?

What you have got to be concerned about is that woman that works in there [at a nuclear facility] for her $12 a month and she has got three kids to feed. That is what you have got to be concerned about because she is going to take it. And she is going to figure out a way of selling it [nuclear material] to feed her kids. That is the danger. And that is a greater danger than any criminals that are already getting fat on controlling everything there. I just had to say that.

Mr. Federmann: Ladies and gentleman, I have been to Russia and to the Soviet Union nine times. The first time, in 1967, I met Anastas Mikoyan. They were already corrupted then. Corrupted up on the 12th floor in the building, not at the eighth floor where you made the business. Then, since 1991, I have been several times to Russia. If I would give the names, the gentleman would say unbelievable. I was a government guest at the Raddison. If I would tell you the names of the people I have been introduced to in Russia and worked with, you would not believe it. And one floor downstairs, already, my people got corrupt, and I had to take them all back. I had one of the biggest Swiss high tech companies with me.

How do you think we will repair this? Only one way, ignore it. Why are the planes are so full? Why can we not get a seat to Moscow? Give me the answer.

Mr. Murphy: I would say that, if you think I explained something here today, you must have misread me. My goal was to get by the whole day without explaining anything.

Mr. de Borchgrave: Claire, do you want to take a crack at this?

Ms. Sterling: Yes, I would like to take a crack at the planes being full. I think that we cannot leave the Russians alone to solve this problem. It is too late for that. I am not sure we can help them solve the problem either. It may be too late for that as well.

But I think the first indispensable element of dealing with this problem is to face it. That is, public knowledge, understanding what has been allowed to happen in Russia and what is happening in Russia is absolutely indispensable to any hope of ever solving the problem. That means confronting the government of Russia head-on and saying, you have to know that we know. This is something that has not yet occurred, as far as I can tell, from any source—at least from our State Department or any source on the Hill, certainly not from the political establishment as such.

I think that has been our first primary sin. We have never said to the Russians (who everybody who knows the situation agrees are corrupt from the top down), "You must know that we know." And that we know does not mean some secret little office in Langley, but that the public knows, the establishment knows, Congress knows. Starting from there, we can try to make an effort to help by offering not money, but technical assistance, collaboration in any form that is acceptable to the Russians.

I am not sure, at this stage, how much will be acceptable to the Russians. I do fear—as others have pointed out here before me today—that any effort on our part, starting with the FBI's own office in Moscow, to make a show of attempting to achieve closer collaboration and exchange of information is more and more likely—given the political situation in Russia—to be interpreted as an effort by the United States to colonize Russia, or at least to take over or dominate or insinuate ourselves into their military establishment and, if possible, its economy.

I am afraid to say I think the situation is very close to hopeless, and it requires brains a lot better than mine to address the problem, starting right away.

Mr. Grinenko: I think that Europe is using Russia at the moment to boost its economy. Europe is giving credits galore, Germany in particular, to the former Soviet Union. That money is coming back and boosting the economy in their own country, whether it be Germany, England, France, all these ...

Ms. Sterling: Illegal money is coming back.

Mr. Grinenko: Besides illegal money. Legal money also—in credits. That is a problem. So nobody is going to change anything.

As far as helping Russia, yes, we should buy all their bombs. That is a solution, is it not?

Question: This is part comment and part question. A year ago I wound up doing business in one of the autonomous regions, Yakutia. I spent a lot of time, not being experienced in doing business in Russia, trying to find out how to do business there. One of the things that was never done by any of the agencies with whom I dealt was for somebody to sit across the table and tell me I would likely be faced with a corrupt administration, with corrupt officials, with corrupt businessmen. I am a kid off the streets of New York. I would know how to deal with that. They let me represent my company in a situation where I was assured they were business people like any other. And, in a strange sort of way, I wound up aiding and abetting them because it took a while for me to figure out how corrupt they were.

Why is not information like I have heard here today more widely available to

American businessmen in advance so they do not wind up inadvertently becoming part of the problem rather than part of the solution? The American businessman is left in the dark.

Ms. Sterling: I would like to add one point. Last year 167,000 visas were issued to Russians as business visas without one of them being screened. Of course, it is a big problem to screen 167,000 applications for visas just in Moscow and St. Petersburg alone, not counting the other ex-Soviet republics. I do not know what the CIA position may be or what advice they give, but clearly the State Department was concerned not to interfere with the development of business relations and trade between the emerging free market of Russia and the United States and, therefore, did not want anything that would slow the process of bringing these people here.

Now, many of them might turn out to be very good and useful and helpful businessmen, but there are a lot of crooks who have come among them as well.

Mr. Grinenko: This is just another little area that Claire and I disagree on. I invited 10 people over last year, business people, and all 10 were denied visas. So this might not be the brightest thing that they do, but they do screen occasionally.

Why they deny, I have no idea, nor did I care any more because it will just be a bureaucratic mess. But they do. And you are right. You are absolutely right. There should be better screening. There is a businessman's office in the embassy or near the embassy in Moscow. They do not tell you these problems. But then again, you have to be a little familiar with the country. I mean, you do not go into business with somebody that does not own the plant, does not have anything in his pocket to put in there. I mean, I did that. And a gentleman once told me, never go into business or do business with anybody that does not have the same amount of interest in it out of his own pocket. And nobody in Russia does.

Question: First, a comment. I wonder how much of what we have been discussing comes from the fact that our government knows how to relate to other governments in a formal sense, that is what our entire government structure for dealing overseas is about. Really what we are confronted with here is a territory without a government, that has a kind of facade of government that does not connect with anything but what it can steal?

Mr. Grinenko: That is right.

Question: And we do not know how to deal with that because we are not structured to deal with terra incognita. It is just ungovernable.

Mr. Grinenko: Yes, but it is to our benefit to get the money.

Ms. Sterling: Well, it depends on who you give the money to.

Question: First, I want to express my appreciation to you, Peter, for explaining why it has been so dangerous to ride in taxis in New York. But then I want to ask you why it is that the Russians, who are so disorganized, got control of the New York gasoline business and stole every dime of New York state and federal revenues.

Mr. Grinenko: You are getting into mismanagement. A little misinformation, too.

First of all, the gasoline scamming was by the Italians. They have always done it. They have done it in a small fashion. Nobody bothered them. And you check all the other states that could have changed their laws that have not for I do not know what reason.

I do not know if everybody is familiar with the gasoline scam. They set up phony companies (getting the necessary documents, buying gasoline or buying the terminal where the gasoline comes in), sell gasoline, collect the tax, and do not pay the government. Normal risky business.

That is a little problem you might have in Russia as a businessman. Your partner will be telling you how many taxes he has got to pay. He does not pay a ruble in taxes. It is the Russian mentality. It is like the scam on the health insurance. I do not know if you people are familiar with it. Close to a billion dollars. California has to restructure its whole system as a result of that scam. Two guys, the Skovitch brothers, just got sentenced. It was excellent.

But the gasoline, they just bust out. I mean, it does not take much sense. The Italians started. They were doing it. The Russians grabbed onto it.

Ms. Sterling: Excuse me, Peter, the people in Baku were working that scam before it was introduced.

Mr. Grinenko: They did not have any cars in Baku.

Robert Mullen: I know it is late in the day but I am having a crisis of perception. Are we dealing with organized crime or with a culture?

Mr. Grinenko: Culture.

Dr. Mullen: If it is the latter, then it cannot be beaten with the traditional methods used to fight organized crime.

Mr. Grinenko: Absolutely correct.

Ms. Sterling: I partially disagree. I think certainly the culture is a very important part of it. But what has happened in the last three or four years is not just a cultural problem. Factors have contributed to it, have added on to the base of it, which has made it something more than a cultural problem. It is difficult, perhaps, impossible to break, to restrain. But, one of the things that has helped it to reach the position it has is that it is an international phenomenon in Russia. The organized crime groups within Russia need the other international crime syndicates to be perfectly effective, to work at maximum efficiency, and vice versa. The international crime community has moved in full flood into Russia. It is exploiting its money laundering facilities, but it is also investing. The two work together. One needs the other. And the interaction of the one upon the other has made it possible to reach degrees of wealth and power that might otherwise not have been possible.

Mr. Grinenko: An old Russian once told me on this question of organized crime, he said, Peter, for 70 years we were the most disorganized country in the world. We have organized crime? It is a cultural problem.

The Varied and Many Risks of Global Organized Crime: Wrap-up

Mr. de Borchgrave: You can see from what just happened that CSIS has undertaken a rather daunting task. But under the leadership of our chairman, Bill Webster, and with the very able assistance of our two codirectors who work alongside me, Erik Peterson and Bob Kupperman—and, of course, with the indefatigable efforts of the man you have been dealing with, our coordinator, Frank Cilluffo, Linnea Raine (a CSIS visiting scholar from the Department of Energy), and Debra van Opstal (a CSIS senior fellow in Science and Technology), I am convinced that we are going to make progress. To set you all straight, here is our chairman, Judge Webster, who would like to make a few concluding remarks.

Chairman Webster: My two co-remarkees have delegated the responsibility to me to tell you what you have heard. After the last panel, I feel I may have a little perceptual fatigue at this point, but I think that it has been a very challenging day. I congratulate you for staying with it. We have a very interesting speaker tonight, the DCI himself.

I would like, before we close, to say that simply because Shakespeare said the first thing we must do is kill all the lawyers, it is not necessarily the solution to the organized crime problem. That is the one thing I am certain about today.

But, whether we are dealing with thugs, or gangs, or Mafia, I think it is also clear that something more than loose familial relationships are involved in the challenge ahead, that the capacity for fraud and corruption in Russia is relatively unlimited. And I am giving you my reactions to what I heard today.

Not very much was mentioned except from some of our guests today about the violence in Russia. Claire has written about it. It is substantial and now exceeds (in serious crime in relation to population) our own high record here, which the Russians used to make great sport of.

It is difficult to do business in Russia, and we are dealing with crime in Russia and crime exported from Russia. It is difficult over there. My firm has an office in Russia, and I know in working with them how much importance is placed on the help we can provide in knowing who to talk to or where to go or what may change from day to day. Justice, itself, is very uncertain. Telephone justice is still a rule in Russia, although they do espouse the rule of law.

Telephone justice, for those of you who are not familiar with it, is the telephone call to the judge to indicate what the preferred result should be. That is a problem. It is a problem when you are dealing with criminals and hoping to put them behind bars under a system that does not rely on decrees but hopes ultimately for a rule of law.

We know that we are dealing with the exportation of crime to the United States, and you have heard many people talk about the problems encountered not only in New York but elsewhere in the country. We know that technology is playing an important role in the evolution of organized crime. It is a role filled with speed and confusion, and I found myself at times awestruck at the challenges for those who are trying to detect the use of modern technology to commit fraud and the rapid movement of money (which I know in international currency today exceeds the entire Third World debt).

And speaking of Third World, I think it is important for us always to remember that, while the former Soviet Union once had a first-rate military, it has always been a Third World country economically. And out of that came the black market that I think provided the basis of the organized crime activity that they now experience today unencumbered by the kind of repression that they had previously experienced. And we must deal with that.

I have not much to say about the transmission of nuclear materials, but I think that Director Woolsey will add to what Director Freeh said this morning about our national concerns in that area. The same applies to other methods of mass destruction and to drugs.

The challenge to cooperate with each other, as pointed out by a number of our panelists today as well as by Director Freeh, is a challenge in terms of trust. With those we trust, we can cooperate well. We can share information and occasionally secrets. With those we cannot trust, as Buck Revell pointed out earlier, it is far more difficult in terms of what can be shared, in terms of what sometimes in intelligence is called sources and methods. But we must find a way to build a trustful relationship with those that we can identify within the former Soviet Union whom we believe are earnestly trying to do a job and can be trusted to handle the information.

I recall going to one country south of here some years ago and I could not meet with my counterpart because of the known corruption of that official. That makes it very, very difficult, and I hope that everyone understands the challenge to American law enforcement and intelligence.

I agree very much with what the commission has said about the importance of recognizing that multilateral cooperation is absolutely essential in dealing with global crime. I take some comfort from the fact that for years Italy had a reputation for corruption that it has not entirely outgrown. But, we have (with the help of very dedicated political figures such as President Scalfaro when he was minister of the interior) found a means of identifying those with whom we could work. And the building of self-respect with the police agencies in Italy and the very effective cooperation in which Director Freeh participated over the years has paid rich dividends, and we must work for that.

We must work for professional improvement within our own law enforcement capability. And I will put in a plug, since I have the privilege of doing that up until 6:00 o'clock, to say that Senator Leahy this morning renewed to me privately his endorsement for the bill that is pending before the Congress now to provide mandatory windows, call them chips if you wish, that will permit the continuation of our traditional electronic surveillance in digital and optic technology, which we do not now have the capability of doing.

I will underscore that the present bill gives law enforcement no more authority to act and still ensures that it is subject to the same constraints in terms of getting an appropriate federal court order or showing probable cause. But I can think of nothing more important in our war against organized crime than that we continue to have that capability, carrying it out exactly as we have before under court supervision. I cannot think of a single organized crime case that was not made without some help from court-authorized electronic surveillance. I commend that to your consideration.

We need to improve intelligence. We need to improve cooperation. We need to alert the private sector. Years ago, when I first came on board at the FBI, we were trying to put together a program called DECA, Defense Counter Intelligence Awareness. We sent agents into the private sector, particularly to defense companies, to caution them about the efforts of hostile intelligence services to obtain secrets. We call it technology transfer. In many cases they were laughed away because this seemed like fiction, perhaps a way of keeping special agents at work. And it was not until we brought down some Soviet agents unprotected by federal immunity and tried them in a public courtroom that people began to realize that we had a serious problem.

It seems to me there is something similar about what we are going through today in terms of international organized crime. We have a serious problem. The experts are well aware of it. The law enforcement community is trying to deal with it. But the public itself only reads about it indirectly and in kind of super-hype articles that do not lay out the scope and magnitude of this problem

I hope that what comes out of this conference will be a series of initiatives—in which many of you will participate–that will help to alert the private sector as well as the government sector to the problems that are growing, not shrinking, in this terribly difficult area of great importance to the national security of our country.

Trends in Global Organized Crime: Additional Observations

Robert H. Kupperman
Project Codirector, CSIS

The world has become an increasingly complex interwoven network, including transportation, communications, finance, power distribution, artificial intelligence, virtual reality, and robotics. When combined with advances in technology, the potential for new criminal ventures becomes all too real. This web, whether used for good or evil, is characteristically vulnerable to computer viruses and logic bombs, as well as to conventional ordinance and electromagnetic pulse.

Law enforcement, usually thought of in superficial tactical terms, can no longer be dismissed as less than a full-fledged member of the national security apparatus. A plethora of technical, security, and ethical issues arise. At the center of the U.S. efforts is the so-called super information highway. One must ask if that highway is a bonanza for economic growth or a curse? We face a small example even now—do law enforcement benefits of the "clipper chip" outweigh the individual's guarantee of privacy?

Along with genuine social progress, as well as economic and humanitarian advancement, the prospects of sophisticated criminality have become a stark reality. Global organized crime, which now lacks definition, may place our traditional freedoms under severe test. However global organized crime is formally defined, it will threaten the continuity of all governments and skew our financial and banking systems in negative ways.

Now is the time to think ahead. This conference is the first in series of studies and events intended to encourage that thinking. We must balance our traditional individual freedoms against a potential "Big Brother" and an imagined techno-wonderland that promises too much.

The conduct of law enforcement is vital for its arbitrary applications that will be felt worldwide. The geopolitics are changing rapidly. Today's criminal has access to vast information bases and weaponry. It will take a lot of thinking–not a macho attitude–to understand and effectively deal with the organized crime of the future.

One thing is sure—crime will be sophisticated and subtle.

For those who know me, you realize that I have dealt with counterterrorism for many years. As devastating as terrorism can be, it is dwarfed by global organized crime and its implications. The world changes in ever more dangerous ways. Counterfeit tender used to buy drugs can also be used to buy plutonium. Weapons of mass destruction abound—chemical, radiological, nuclear and biological. Molecular biology, which changes the genetic content of present life forms, can be a boon in reducing human suffering, but it is also a double-edged sword. Man-made diseases can result from molecular tinkering, producing organisms that could ravage the earth. As a result, the tiniest of unstable governments or parliamentary groups could extort the largest of countries.

This brings us 360 degrees around. We are forced to reexamine our legal system and our mores. We must be prepared to answer difficult questions. Evidence of complicity in global organized criminal activity is almost never clear cut enough to stand the rigors of the judicial system. Is it appropriate to remove powerful individuals or even government leaders when they are in fact a part of global organized crime?

This conference, while immensely enlightening to me, has raised far more questions than given answers. But this is the nature of a good conference.

Global Organized Crime: Threats to U.S. and International Security

R. James Woolsey
Director of Central Intelligence

Mr. de Borchgrave: We have all heard a lot today. I think there is a lot of food for thought. We heard from Director Freeh at breakfast. And, just in case you think the FBI is not on the job, I have received a true intercept (and this is not made up, it is not *Saturday Night Live*) that the FBI made of itself while they were conducting an investigation in San Diego. It was sent to me by a friend of mine who used to be with counterintelligence in Washington. It is called "The FBI Pizza Call."

FBI agents conducted a raid of a psychiatric hospital in San Diego that was under investigation for medical insurance fraud. After hours of reviewing thousands of medical records, the dozens of agents worked up quite an appetite. The agent in charge of the investigation called a nearby pizza parlor with delivery service to order a quick dinner for his colleagues. The following telephone conversation took place and was recorded by the FBI because they were taping the hospital.

Agent: "Hello. I would like to order 19 large pizzas and 67 cans of soda."

Pizza Man: "And where would you like them delivered?

Agent: "We're over at the psychiatric hospital."

Pizza Man: "To the psychiatric hospital?"

Agent: "That's right. I'm an FBI agent."

Pizza Man "You're an FBI agent?"

Agent: "That's correct. Just about everybody here is."

Pizza Man: "And you're at the psychiatric hospital?"

Agent: "That's correct. And make sure you don't go through the front doors. We have them locked. You will have to go around to the back to the service entrance to deliver the pizzas."

Pizza Man: "And you say you're all FBI agents?"

Agent: "That's right. How soon can you have them here?"

Pizza Man: "And everyone at the psychiatric hospital is an FBI agent?"

Agent: "That's right. We've been here all day and we're starving."

Pizza Man: "How are you going to pay for all of this?"

Agent: "I have my checkbook right here."

Pizza Man: "And you're all FBI agents?"

Agent: "That's right. Everyone here is an FBI agent. Can you remember to bring the pizzas and sodas to the service entrance in the rear? We have the front doors locked."

Pizza Man: "I don't think so."

Click.

M. de Borchgrave: True story. That is what is funny about it.

Now I would like to bring up our esteemed chairman, Bill Webster, to introduce our guest of honor.

Chairman Webster: Buck Revell assures me that was not the genesis of the Pizza Connection case.

This is a very pleasant and easy assignment for me and for anyone who has spent any time at all in Washington because Jim Woolsey has been a fixture, and important fixture, in this town for well over 20 years. Many of us know that he was a graduate of Stanford; a Rhodes Scholar; attended Yale Law School, where he was the managing editor of the Yale Law Journal; and, then, got himself into the army, where he got his first exposure to national security work as a special adviser on the SALT I talks. In 1970, he was appointed general counsel for the United States Senate Armed Services Committee, where he served until 1973 when he became associated with a Washington law firm. From 1983 to 1986, he served as a delegate at large to the U.S.-Soviet Strategic Arms Reduction Talks (START) and nuclear space talks.

I first became acquainted with Jim, although we had known each other here in Washington, in connection with something called the Aspen Strategy Group, which meets annually at the Aspen Institute to discuss major national policy issues.

Everyone recognizes that Jim has an insightful mind. He is a forceful advocate. And he is a person committed to service to his country. He served as a regent of the Smithsonian, as a trustee at Stanford, and many other areas in which his talents were brought to bear for the good of the institutions that he cares about.

He is just finishing up his first year as director of Central Intelligence, the president's choice, and I want to say that he was everyone else's choice who knew Jim and his prospects there. We had a luncheon shortly before his confirmation hearing, and I assured him that it was a piece of cake, no problems at all.

Well, I am not sure what kind of cake, and he was kind enough not to ask. But, in this challenging time, he has never lost his sense of humor and his belief in the importance of intelligence and of the men and women who serve in it selflessly in the interest of their country. I think it is appropriate that we started with Louis Freeh and close this evening with Jim Woolsey. We have been building up to an important statement.

James Woolsey

Bill, thank you very much. On that piece of cake business, you lied. And, Arnaud, please, someone pass on to Louis Freeh that, contrary to a story that was circulating around our table, my slipping you that transcript was not a covert action by the CIA.

My last government service prior to becoming director of Central Intelligence was as U.S. ambassador to the CFE talks in Vienna. The capitals of Europe have always provided a remarkable setting for negotiations.

In 1992, a year after I left Vienna, the city of Prague served as a backdrop for a different kind of negotiation, a secret negotiation with no government representatives. Discussions were not about arms control or the need to settle regional disputes. This was not the world of NATO, the European Union, or CSCE. This was the world of international organized crime, and the participants were representatives from Italian and Russian organized crime groups. The Italians agreed to provide "know-how" for the acquisition and distribution of illegal drugs, while Russian groups pledged to provide security, along with transit and distribution routes.

In Latin America, powerful drug groups established ad hoc, mutually beneficial arrangements with insurgent or terrorist groups such as the Sendero Luminoso in Peru and the Revolutionary Armed Forces, or FARC, in Colombia. While the relationship between drug dealers and these groups has been contentious at times, insurgents are sometimes paid to provide security services for drug traffickers, they often "tax" drug operations in areas they control, and in some instances, they are directly involved in narcotics cultivation.

In Africa, criminal groups based in Nigeria continue to work around the clock to arrange transshipments of heroin from Thailand through Lagos and onto Europe. These same enterprises are responsible for shipping 30 to 40 percent of all the heroin coming into the United States. They are also involved in massive credit card fraud. The Financial Crimes Division of the Secret Service estimates that they account for more than $2.5 million in credit card fraud a month in Dallas alone.

In Russia, President Yeltsin warned earlier this year that organized crime had become the number one problem facing Russia. In terms of reported crimes, however, official Baltic and Commonwealth of Independent States statistics ranked Russia third per capita among former Soviet Republics, behind Estonia and Latvia. Estonia's murder rate is among the highest in the world, and Latvian Interior Ministry officials estimate that as much as one-fourth to one-half of the Latvian economy is associated with organized crime. The leaders of these countries, along with Eduard Shevardnadze in Georgia and other leaders throughout the former Soviet Union, are plagued by organized crime and corruption, which are eating away at economic and political reforms.

Let me be blunt. These examples demonstrate that the threat from organized crime transcends traditional law enforcement concerns. They affect critical national security interests. While organized crime is not a new phenomenon today, some governments find their authority besieged at home and their foreign policy interests imperiled abroad. Drug trafficking, links between drug traffickers and terrorists, smuggling of illegal aliens, massive financial and bank fraud, arms smuggling, potential involvement in the theft and sale of nuclear material, political intimidation and corruption all constitute a poisonous brew—a mixture potentially as deadly as some of what we faced during the cold war. Let me sketch for you the magnitude of the problem.

Organized crime is a multibillion dollar transnational business. Profits from drug trafficking alone—some $200 billion to $300 billion a year—dwarf the GNP of virtually all the 170 nations in the international system.

Organized crime is a sophisticated business. The Cali cartel uses market assessments to guide its operations, buys commercially available state-of-the-art communications to support its international transaction, and it even studies trade patterns to plan its transportation of illegal cocaine. It also places great emphasis on developing and maintaining sophisticated money laundering operations for its huge profits.

Organized crime can undermine the sovereignty of a state, although criminal groups do not deliberately set out to do so. Indeed, their preference is to ignore the country they operate in. But when threatened by law enforcement, these groups respond with every means available, from bribery to murder, to protect their operations.

There is one major difference between how we have dealt with the more traditional threats to our national security and how we handle the threats from organized crime: the tools of diplomacy are ineffective and irrelevant in dealing directly with these criminal groups. Even under the most difficult, intractable period of the cold war, if consensus was not possible, communication was, nevertheless, feasible. Not so in the world of organized crime. Although we do negotiate with our key allies and friends to better attack the problem of organized crime, there is no negotiating table where we can try to work out a compromise or reach a consensus with criminals, with those whose particular brand of diplomacy includes drug trafficking, extortion, and murder. Negotiations, diplomatic démarches, Security Council resolutions, fact-finding missions, or peacekeeping forces play no role in this shadowy and violent world.

Tonight I want to talk to you about two important dimensions of the threat from international organized crime. The first is a threat posed by international drug trafficking, a logical place to start inasmuch as drug trafficking is the international criminal activity with the most serious impact on societies—and the most substantial moneymaker for criminal enterprises. Second, I want to talk to you about organized crime in Russia—an issue of growing importance to President Yeltsin—and to all of us here who are committed to supporting the positive transformations that have been unfolding in the aftermath of the collapse of the Soviet Union.

At first glance there does not seem to be an obvious connection between these two problems, but in both instances, the ability of governments to implement their agendas is at risk. The local economy, economic and political reform, the viability of democratic government, and the trust between the electorate and the elected can all be jeopardized by the grip of organized crime. In parts of Latin America the profits from drug trafficking already have enabled criminal organizations to buy elections, politicians, and government officials—in short, to subvert democratic processes and undermine fragile governments. The situation in Russia has not reached that point, and drug trafficking does not dominate the economic life of that country. But a panoply of organized criminal behavior does pose a danger to President Yeltsin's hopes and plans to advance fundamental political and economic reform for the betterment of the Russian people.

Let me begin with drug trafficking. Drug trafficking has created a crisis that spans the globe—and it's growing. We are all aware that Latin American narcotics traffickers control the massive and profitable worldwide cocaine trade. The Cali cartel has evolved into the world's most powerful trafficking syndicate. It has demonstrated a great deal of resiliency, changing trafficking and security operations to blunt threats either from rival drug groups or from counternarcotics forces. It has also demonstrated a great deal of flexibility, expanding to take advantage of new "products"—in this case, smuggling heroin into the United States—and new markets, exporting cocaine to Europe.

One could look at how drug traffickers are developing and sustaining the European market for cocaine as a model of a successful multinational business. Latin American groups know that Italian and other European groups control the drug distribution networks in Europe, networks built up over 40 years to accommodate the flow of heroin. Italian groups know that cocaine is increasing in popularity in Europe. And both groups know that cocaine sells in Europe for two to three times the U.S.

price, meaning that there are enormous profits to be made.

As a result, Latin American groups provide the drugs, using groups in Venezuela, Brazil, and Argentina to transship cocaine to newer markets in Europe, while distribution remains in the hands of European—primarily Italian—organized crime.

Thus the "virtual corporation" touted by management theorists as the leading contender for the dominant entrepreneurial structure of the next century takes shape: drug traffickers develop a loose network of independent companies; they share information, skills, costs, and market access and position themselves to pool their relative strengths in order to take advantage of emerging markets throughout the globe.

The problem of international drug trafficking is not limited to cocaine. Heroin production and distribution continues to flow unabated, primarily from Southeast and southwest Asia. Although most of the opium produced in Asia is actually consumed there, more than half of the refined product available on the U.S. market comes from Southeast Asia. Ethnic Chinese groups—sometimes called Triads—are involved in an array of criminal enterprises. But what sustains these triads is the key role they play in transshipping Southeast Asian heroin through Hong Kong, Taiwan, and Singapore.

Southwest Asia—primarily Afghanistan and Pakistan—is home to large poppy seed cultivation. Most of the southwest Asian heroin that is consumed in the West transits through Turkey from where it flows into distribution networks in Europe—where Italian organized crime groups are the major players in the drug trade—and into the United States.

The debilitating effect of international drug trafficking cannot be overstated. I mentioned the ad hoc arrangements between drug traffickers and insurgents and terrorists. In addition, drug trafficking drives up exponentially the rate of violent crime and political corruption and can devastate significant sectors of a country's national economy.

For example, leaders of the Cali cartel have manipulated the political and legal system of several Latin American countries. Lawyers working for the Cali cartel helped shape Colombia's legislative reform of the legal system, whose very provisions the kingpins have been using to gain easy plea bargaining agreements.

Violence is an accepted part of drug trafficking—against one another, against government and law enforcement officials and members of the judiciary, and even against those who have spoken out against traffickers. Earlier this year an Italian priest in Naples who had urged his parishioners to shun the Camorra criminal organization was murdered in his church while preparing for mass.

The inflow of funds wreaks havoc with local economies as well. In Colombia and Venezuela, for example, displacement of legitimate business from key sectors of the economy such as agriculture, construction, and tourism continues as a result of launderer-controlled companies' using their drug money to undercut their competitors.

As I said at the beginning of my remarks, drug traffickers have forged links with Russian organized crime. But drug trafficking is not the sole activity of business for these Russian groups. They are also involved in the sale of weapons, antiques, icons, raw materials, stolen vehicles, and even some radioactive materials, and they make concerted efforts to gain influence—and as much control as they can—over Russia's growing banking and private sectors.

To understand the magnitude of Russian organized crime, we have to dismiss two ideas at the outset. First, it is not organized or monolithic in the sense of a single "Mafia"—despite the tendency of Russians to use that term when referring to organized crime. Indeed the recent assassinations of dozens of high-level criminal leaders belies the notion of a single, stable structure based on cooperation. Second, organized crime in Russia is not a new phenomenon. The criminal establishment there —what Russians refer to as "thieves within the law"—existed throughout the life of the 74-year-old Soviet state. Some of its activities were tolerated and even encouraged by the Communist Party because its members often stood to gain from its black market operations.

When the Soviet Union collapsed, these groups found themselves in a freer environment within which to pursue their criminal activities. They have exploited economic dislocations, relaxation of social controls, diffusion and decentralization of power, opening up of borders, and the transfer of the states' wealth to private hands.

The groups that had found a niche under the old system operated within a clearly defined code of behavior. The Soviet state could halt criminal activities that went beyond acceptable limits—such as dabbling in the trade of nuclear materials. Leaders could be threatened with imprisonment and their operation shut down if they overstepped the bounds set by the state. Some of those who were imprisoned even honed their criminal entrepreneurial skills in the Soviet Gulag.

Today, all of this has changed. Not only are the illegal activities that characterized the Soviet period spilling over borders in Europe and the rest of the world, but organized crime and corruption in and around Russia are working to weaken the political and economic system that President Yeltsin is working to create and that the West is supporting politically and economically.

Although the old code is gone, the old groups survive and thrive. They are also competing with new groups formed by former and even some current government bureaucrats who learned how to manipulate the defects of the old system to their own advantage and who have joined existing, or have created new, criminal organizations.

Perhaps most dangerous are groups of former military personnel and security service officers who provide protection to criminal leaders and collect protection payments. Trained to defend the interests of the Soviet state, these individuals have now offered their services to protect the interests of crime lords by engaging in criminal warfare. Declining morale, poor living conditions, erratic or late pay, poor prospects either for advancement within the military or for a better life outside the military, all these work to make military personnel particularly susceptible to offers from organized crime groups. These individuals not only bring their expertise, but often military equipment as well. Theft and illegal sales of weapons and other military stocks have become troublingly frequent.

Corruption also extends from traffic police, customs officials, and border guards up to the highest levels of the law enforcement and security community. An official of the Interior Ministry said that last year alone more than 500 staffers were dismissed for selling police information to criminals.

Today, criminal groups operate in virtually every city and region of the Russian Federation, carving up criminal spheres along geographic and functional lines. The numbers cited by the Russian government are daunting. According to the Russian Ministry of Internal Affairs, there are 5,700 organized crime groups in Russia, of which 200 are large, sophisticated organizations. Over 100 of these conduct operations throughout Russia and in 29 countries.

Because of Russia's challenge to develop a viable banking system to help sustain economic reform, the banking and financial sectors are particularly vulnerable to threats from organized crime. Interior Ministry officials estimate that organized crime controls most of Russia's 2,000 banks and over half of its financial capital, although the definition of "control" varies from owning and operating these institutions, to providing financial information to criminal groups under threat of extortion of violence.

The privatization effort is also under attack from organized crime. Russian officials believe that criminals are involved in roughly 40,000 state and private enterprises. Criminal groups are reported to have controlled about one-third of the turnover in goods and services in 1993. According to Russian Customs officials, the illegal export of raw materials alone reportedly costs the Russian government $10 billion in lost revenues per year.

Moreover, protection payments have become a standard cost of doing business in Russia—for Russians and for foreign business. Last month three racketeers even hijacked a car from the *Newsweek* bureau in Moscow, demanding protection money. They assumed that the power of the press was monetary.

An ominous development to this rise in organized crime is the propensity of these groups to settle economic and political disputes through contract assassinations—murder for hire. Over the last two years, criminals have brazenly murdered high-level political officials as well as dozens of influential businessmen and bankers.

In this environment, we are particularly concerned with the safety of nuclear, chemical, and biological materials as well as highly enriched uranium or plutonium and the potential for its falling into the hands of organized crime groups.

Russian criminal organizations have the extensive infrastructure—built on ties to corrupt military, political, and law enforcement officials—which could be used to facilitate the transfer and sale of these weapons or these materials. They also have the resources to bribe or threaten those who handle such material into cooperating with them.

But let me point out that, despite considerable press speculation to the contrary, trading in nuclear weapons and materials is not the primary or even secondary source of business today for these criminal enterprises. The other avenues for crime— extortion, financial fraud, narcotics trafficking—are far too profitable for the established criminal groups to abandon them for the high risk goal of stealing weapons of mass destruction. But we can ill afford to assume that because brokering such transactions has not yet been an activity of such groups, we can relax our guard and remain confident that such a contingency would never occur. After all, there is no shortage of customers—Iran, Iraq, Libya would pay dearly for such expertise. For example, we estimate that Iran is about 8 to 10 years away from developing a nuclear capability and has sought ways to short circuit the timetable through the purchase of such material from Russia. President Yeltsin made clear his view on the importance of ensuring the safety and security of these weapons when he publicly stated, "The proliferation of nuclear and other categories of weapons of mass destruction within the country and beyond cannot be allowed."

In an address last May to the members of the Russian Federation Counterintelligence Service, President Yeltsin warned that "the criminalization of society is continuing." This then is the reality of organized crime in Russia.

Comparisons between the gang wars of Chicago in the 1920s and the activities of organized crime groups in Moscow and elsewhere in Russia are misleading. As violent as some of our gang wars were, the fabric of American democracy was never called into question. The same cannot be said of Russia. The president and all of us who work on these matters in the U.S. government support the efforts to combat organized crime in Russia for one fundamental reason: The success or failure of President Yeltsin and the Russian government in meeting this threat will affect both the future of Russia and the national security interests of the United States.

President Yeltsin and the Russian government are taking extensive action to counter this threat. In May, President Yeltsin signed the federal anti-crime program, which calls for new laws, greater centralization of units within the Interior Ministry to increase their effectiveness, improved monitoring of banking transactions, and a heightened military police presence. President Yeltsin followed up one month later by signing another decree—one that attracted much debate—that granted law enforcement agencies greater investigative power such as searching homes, businesses, and records of individuals suspected of organized criminal activity and that allowed the police to detain suspects for 30 days with no formal charges. President Yeltsin also authorized transferring up to 52,000 men from the military to assist law enforcement agencies.

The implications for President Yeltsin's reforms—and for the West—are enormous. Russian criminal organizations not only threaten government authority, in some instances they are viewed by citizens as alternatives to state authority because of the services they provide: security in the form of protection of individuals and property; arbitration in the form of settling disputes or seeing that business contracts are honored; financial assistance in the form of loans, often at lower rates than banks; and even some social services such as assistance to the needy through criminally owned philanthropic organizations. President Yeltsin does not want the first generation of Russians to come of age free of the oppression of the Soviet state, only to view as natural the idea of relying on criminal organizations as opposed to the state to settle disputes or provide essential services.

To help in the battle against organized crime—whether in Latin America or in the former Soviet Union—we need three critical ingredients.

First, we need the utmost cooperation between the worlds of law enforcement and intelligence, a view shared by Attorney General Reno, FBI Director Freeh, and other leaders in both communities. We cannot afford to view law enforcement and intelligence as an "either or" proposition. We need the active cooperation of both if we hope to combat and defeat organized crime.

Second, we need the utmost cooperation among America's allies and friends. President Yeltsin and President Clinton are discussing how to work most effectively in partnership to counter these criminal threats. In addition, traditional links with intelligence and law enforcement counterparts with our key allies must be expanded. Moreover, we need to develop further such links with our new friends in Eastern Europe and with other successor states of the former Soviet Union.

Third, we need to be smart, creative, flexible—and determined. The list of topics you addressed today cover the gamut from financial fraud to smuggling of fissile materials. The fight against organized crime is demanding and painstaking: tracing the trail of money being laundered through three continents; piecing together the assembly and shipment of weapons through front companies; unraveling links between the Cali cartel, the Italian Mafia, and Russian criminal groups; or interpreting the local dialects used by the Chinese Triads. To do all of this, to be able to uncover organized criminal enterprises, and to track and even to anticipate their moves, we will need to make use of our best asset in the world of intelligence: our people. Our linguists, scientists, engineers, financial analysts, economists, and historians must work to ferret out plans and, with their law enforcement counterparts, to attack organized crime across its entire chain of command.

Within the CIA itself I have directed our Counternarcotics Center to take on expanded responsibilities in the fight against international organized crime. The Center, which will be renamed the Crime and Narcotics Center, will be responsible for providing intelligence support to policymakers and law enforcement officials on organized crime. It will include a newly formed Organized Crime Target Analysis Group to provide intelligence on the infrastructure of major international organized crime groups and to cover vulnerabilities in their operations. We will also be establishing within this Center an expanded financial crimes unit to target international money laundering activities of both international narcotics and other organized crime groups.

In addition, last year I established in the National Intelligence Council the position of National Intelligence Officer for Global and Multilateral Affairs. In this position, Doctor Enid Shottle oversees the drafting of estimates on a whole range of critical issues that transcend national borders—such as the growing menace of organized crime. But this position entails more than producing these estimates. It involves bringing together the analytical talent found not only throughout the intelligence community but throughout the government: at the Justice and State Departments and at the FBI.

We know from past experience that victory against organized crime will not come as dramatically as the fall of the Berlin Wall or the liberation of Kuwait. Victory will be measured by the plots uncovered, the plans thwarted, the connections disrupted. And we in the intelligence community will be judged by how well we have helped others in their struggle to protect the basis of democratic government, the faith between the citizens and the leaders they elect.

Appendix

L. Dain Gary   **Carnegie Mellon University**
                          Pittsburgh, Pennsylvania

What is CERT?

Formed in 1988 by DARPA

Mission:

- **facilitate and coordinate responses to computer security events**
- **raise community's awareness and understanding**
- **conduct research**

Incident Response Activities

Help the Internet community respond to computer security incidents

Maintain incident data in secure repository

Facilitate communications between sites, response teams, investigators, and vendors

Maintain expert knowledge in technologies being exploited

Carnegie Mellon University

CERT's Constituency-Internet

Global distribution

- **30,500 smaller networks and service providers**

Multitude of technologies

- **3,140,000 host computers**

Diverse user demographics

- **government agencies**

- **academic and research institutions**

- **corporate users**

Carnegie Mellon University

CERT's 1993 Experiences

73% increase over 1992 levels

- **111 new computer security incidents a month**

39% increase in the number of sites affected

- **incidents have involved from 1 to over 65,000 sites**

19 CERT Advisories published

CERT's 1994 Experiences

77% increase over 1993 levels

- **195 new computer security incidents a month**

51% increase in the number of sites affected

13 CERT Advisories published

Typical Network Attack Scenario

1) Locate system to attack using information provided by a hacker bulletin board or network information center, or by using a locator function (e.g., the UNIX nslookup function)

2) Find a weak password on an unprivileged account on one machine connected to a network, and break in

3) Use a vulnerability in the system's operating system to gain privileged status

4) Disable accounting

5) Read e-mail and/or transfer files (of <u>any</u> user in the system)

6) Jump to another system, and repeat previous steps

Carnegie Mellon University

Types of incidents

• Malicious code

- Viruses, worms, Trojan horses, time bombs, pests

• Procedural failures, improper acts

- Transmitting sensitive information without knowing the safeguards in the receiving system.

• Intrusions (break-ins)

- Authentication bypass

- Attacks using provided services (e.g., sendmail, finger, rsh, etc.)

- Snooping attacks (wiretapping, network monitoring, electronic monitoring of CRTs)

• Insider attacks

• Espionage

Carnegie Mellon University

Changes in Intrusion Profile

1988
- exploiting passwords
- exploiting known vulnerabilities

1994
- exploiting passwords
- exploiting known vulnerabilities
    - sendmail
- exploiting protocol flaws
- installing snooping programs
    - modifying network programs
    - collecting network traffic for examination
- examining source files for new security flaws
- icmp attacks
- anonymous FTP abuse

Carnegie Mellon University

Possible Effects of an Attack

- Denial of service
    - Network jamming
    - Introducing fraudulent packets
    - System crashes/poor performance
- Unauthorized use or misuse of computing systems
- Loss/alteration/compromise of data or software
- Loss of money (e.g., embezzlement, theft, cost of restoring systems, etc.)
- Loss or endangerment of human life
- Loss of trust in computer / network system
- Loss of public confidence

Carnegie Mellon University

Top Five Incident Types

The following top five types are based on incident information reported to CERT.

Trusted system attacks
TFTP attacks
Network Information Services (NIS) attacks
Network File System (NFS) attacks
Password attacks

Carnegie Mellon University

CERT's Expanded Program

Incident response, while necessary, <u>is not sufficient!</u>

CERT has evolved to a more comprehensive program designed to help reduce network vulnerabilities and prevent security incidents.

The major thrust of this expanded program is to improve

- networked systems security technology

- networked systems security practice

Carnegie Mellon University

Improving Technology

Increase vendor sensitivity to security requirements

- **Improve existing products**
- **Influence future products**

Conduct research in computer security incident handling

Improving Security Practice

Focused education and training programs designed to:
- **Increase overall awareness of security needs**
- **define management's role in system security**
- **improve security policies and procedures**
- **improve system administration**
  - **configuration**
  - **maintenance**

Site specific security improvement programs

Why the increased emphasis?

- Corporate dependence on computers
- Increased use of networks
- Technological sophistication of equipment
- Distribution of the computer security function
- Number of adversaries is increasing
- More sophisticated cracking tools

 CERT **Carnegie Mellon University**

Computer Security Risk Multipliers

- Denial of problem by management
- Absence of effective, well-distributed, and enforced policies and procedures
- Direct Internet connections
- System management problems
- System administration problems
- Lack of necessary technical expertise

CERT **Carnegie Mellon University**

Observations

We still see too many people who think security is "somebody else's job." - Responsibility <u>must</u> be fixed!

Although tougher security edicts cannot prevent hacker attacks, corporate managers must do a better job of enforcing basic system safeguards...

Too much of the problem is still kept in the closet because of the political or financial embarrassment.

Carnegie Mellon University

CERT: Contact Information

24-hour telephone: **(412) 268-7090**

FAX: **(412) 268-6989**

Electronic Mail: **cert@cert.org**

U.S. Mail: **CERT**
Software Engineering Institute
Carnegie Mellon University
Pittsburgh, PA 15213-3890

THE WILD WEST OF NETSEC — BETWEEN WARNING AND DISASTER

By:

Donn B. Parker

June 1994

QUOTES

"We are in the golden age between warning and disaster".

- Stuart Brand

"Give me $1 billion and 20 people and I'll shut America Down".

- Senior Intelligence Official

"We are going to see info-terrorism, not just by hackers playing games, but by countries, criminal syndicates".

- Alvin Toffler

"Information people are mostly techies who believe that information and technology are mental, everything they do is objective rather than tinged with subjectivity".

- Alvin Toffler

THE CHANGING NATURE OF BUSINESS LOSSES

- Same Losses by Name
  - Fraud
  - Sabotage
  - Errors and omissions
  - Fire, flood, contamination

- New Loss Factors
  - Occupations of perpetrators
  - Environments
  - Methods
  - Fragile assets
  - Timing and geography

Spectrum of Loss Sources

- Natural forces
- Human error
- Hackers and phreaks
- Amateur white-collar criminals
- Career criminals

CHANGES IN FREQUENCY OF BUSINESS CRIME

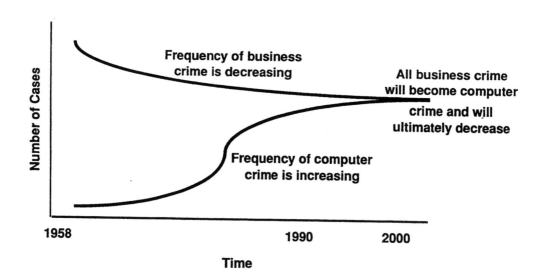

CHANGES IN BUSINESS CRIME LOSS PER CASE

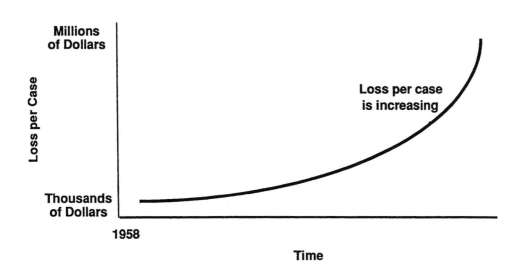

A HISTORY OF COMPUTER CRIMOIDS

Crimoids: Criminal method that receives brief, intense publicity, with catastrophic loss potential and variable actual effect

1970s	1980s	1990s
Privacy violations	Electronic letter bomb	Specific computer viruses
Salami round-down fraud	Software piracy	PBX toll fraud
Phone phreak toll fraud	Radio frequency eavesdropping	
Wire tapping		
Hacker trespass		

What Is Next?

Computer larceny	Automated hacking
Desk top forgery	EDI fraud
Phantom nodes in networks	

FUTURE OF COMPUTER CRIMOIDS

FUTURE COMPUTER CRIMOIDS	CONTROLS
• **Computer larceny** Stealing computers and stored information	• **Jewelry security**
• **Automated hacking** Sniffers, subverted utility programs	• **Firewalls, monitoring**
• **Desktop forgery** Business documents and tickets	• **Electronic data interchange**
• **Information anarchy** Absolute privacy destruction of privacy from uncontrolled crypto	• **Escrowed strong crypto**
• **Internet abuse** Extreme advocacy groups usage	• **Change values, enforce laws**
• **LANarchy** Phantom nodes and paths	• **Inventory LANs**
• **International industrial espionage** Moles, social engineering, and dichotomy of ethical values	• **Multilateral - agreements**
• **Electronic data interchange (EDI) fraud** Forgery, counterfeiting, misrepresentation, and repudiation	• **Electronic signatures**

COMPLETE LIST OF ACCIDENTAL AND INTENTIONAL THREATS TO INFORMATION

➤ **Threats to Availability and Usefulness**
   Destroy, damage, or contaminate
   Deny, prolong, or delay use or access

➤ **Threats to Integrity and Authenticity**
   Enter, use, or produce false data
   Modify, replace, or reorder
   Misrepresent
   Repudiate
   Misuse or fail to use as required

➤ **Threats to Confidentiality and Possession**
   Access
   Disclose
   Observe or monitor
   Copy
   Steal

➤ **Exposure to Threats**
   Endanger by exposure to any of the above threats

Dynamics of the Hacker Culture

- Increase of pre-hackers, 9-12 years old, motivated by:

  —Peer and mentor approval
  —Short cut to education and lowered expectation of achieving higher education
  —Curiosity
  —More powerful tools but limited access
  —Pre-teenage syndrome
  —Introduction to computers and data communication
  —Lack of parental understanding, guidance, control

- Hackers, 12-18 years old, already addicted, hardened, committed

- Hackers, 18 years old, face adult prosecution and some end the practice, others engage only vicariously through others

- Hackers, 18-24 years leave to take up responsible lives

MALICIOUS HACKER PROFILE

- Persistence, curiosity, challenged
- Routinely lie, cheat, steal, exaggerate, deceive
- Juvenile idealism:
  - Power to the people
  - Information and services must be free for those who know how to use them
  - Don't harm people, couldn't steal from people
  - If it feels good, do it
  - A quick way to a great career, all fun and no work
  - Attack systems to force management to make them secure
  - Vendors should publicly reveal their product vulnerabilities and fix them
- Hyperactive, unable to sit in class
- Drugs and alcohol
- Sexually vulnerable, pedophile targets

THE HACKER SOCIETY

- Disdain clubs or organizations
- Commercial efforts: 2600, Phrack, Hactic, CHAOS
- Groups formed, merged, disbanded quickly
- Top hacker groups: ZARGOZ(100), CORE(35) by invitation
- Anonymity, intrigues, liaisons
- Meritocracy-rise in stature based on knowledge
- Play at commerce
- Old culture seeks knowledge, public service, destitution, anarchy, esthetics
- New culture seeks profits, work for pay, use of moles, business, tools
- Electronic wars and battles
- All believe in avoiding harm to the PSN
- Believe the tabloids and spread misinformation

HACKER'S SECURITY CRUSADE

- Use moles or "friends" in vendor companies
- Use social engineering, trashing, purchased manuals
- Great disdain for most vendors and customers
- Want immediate public vulnerability reporting and fixing
- Complaints about CERT secretiveness
- Great respect for Kerberos, RSA crypto, tokens
- Intent to help achieve better security
  - Ignored, rebuffed
  - Confused and hurt
  - Retribution follows

HACKER SUBJECTS OF INTEREST

- **Top hackers (25 in the USA)**
  - **Bring down PSN switch through software**
  - **Cause disastrous PSN disruption**
  - **Destroy confidence in PSN through access**
- **Black hats**
  - **Regularly, maliciously hack networks and computers**
- **Grey hats**
  - **Hold infotech or network jobs or consult**
  - **Maintain active contact with hacker community**
  - **May do some hacking**
- **White hats**
  - **Infotech and network technologies**
  - **Fighting against hacker intrusions**
  - **Claim no contact with hacker community**

FINDINGS: THE HACKER CULTURE, COMPLETED

- **EASTERN EUROPEAN HACKERS A NEW AND OMINOUS CONCERN**
  - **NO CURRENT THREAT NOW BECAUSE OF LACK OF ADEQUATE ACCESS TO U.S. PSN**

  - **FUTURE THREAT:**

    U.S. PSN WILL BECOME ACCESSIBLE AS NATIONAL PSN INFRASTRUCTURES IMPROVE

    NATIONAL ECONOMIC PROBLEMS COULD FUEL ANGER, FRUSTRATION, BASIC AS MOTIVATIONS FOR MALICIOUS HACKING

  - **RUSSIA: SOURCE OF VERY LARGE NUMBER OF TRAINED COMPUTER SCIENTISTS**

  - **BULGARIA: SOURCE OF EXCEPTIONALLY VIRULENT VIRUSES**

SOME OF SRI'S CONCLUSIONS AND RECOMMENDATIONS

1. GENERAL CONCLUSIONS

- NO EVIDENCE OF DETERMINED EFFORT TO SABOTAGE THE ENTIRE PSN BY CURRENT GENERATION OF HACKERS

- MOTIVATION OF HACKERS IS CHANGING; NEW GENERATION INTERESTED IN FINANCIAL GAIN CHANGES THE GAME ENTIRELY

- NOT POSSIBLE TO STOP DETERMINED PEOPLE FROM HACKING INTO THE PSN; IS POSSIBLE TO MAKE IT MORE DIFFICULT TO DO

- FOUR MAJOR AREAS OF CONCERN HAVE LITTLE OR NOTHING TO DO WITH TECHNICAL VULNERABILITIES OF THE PSN:

    - SUSCEPTIBILITY OF TELCO EMPLOYEES TO SOCIAL ENGINEERS
    - LAX PHYSICAL AND PROCEDURAL ACCESS CONTROLS
    - ACCESSIBILITY OF CRITICAL INFORMATION FROM TRASHING
    - PRESENCE OF MOLES IN TELCOS, SUPPLIER COMPANIES, ETC.

- HACKERS NOW RECEPTIVE TO SRI'S PROBING AND RESEARCH

NCS

SRI   19

Possible Solutions to the Hacker Problem

1. **Increase infosec against hackers**
    —Emphasis on confrontational and detection controls
    —Systems and human prevention controls will never be fully successful
    —Eliminate the "beat the system" challenge

2. **Employ the means of law**
    —Vigorous criminal and civil litigation
    —Increase sanctions
    —Strengthen rules of evidence
    —Improve search and seizure

3. **Interdict the hacker life cycle**
    —Deter entry into the culture
    —Rely on attrition to reduce population

- **Resistance, sanctions, downsize**

Air Force Office of Special Investigations

Countering the Computer Intrusion Threat

Special Agent Jim Christy
Director, Computer Crime Investigations
Investigative Operations Center

OSI Computer Crime Investigations

The Problem - On-Line Vulnerability Testing Results:

   - Gain Privilege on 88% of Systems Tested

   - Only 4% of the Victims Know They Have Been Attacked

OSI Computer Crime Investigations

OSI's Counterintelligence Investigative Jurisdiction:
- **AF Interest Systems**
- **Defense Logistics Agency**
- **Defense Security Assistance Agency**
- **Ballistic Missile Defense Office**
- **Office of the Secretary of Defense**

OSI Computer Crime Investigations

Hacker Investigation Uniqueness

The Hacker NEVER has to be Anywhere Near the Crime Scene

The Hacker Usually Will Have Multiple Victims Simultaneously

The AF is Rarely the Sole Target of the Hacker

Usually Involve Multiple Investigative Jurisdictions

OSI Computer Crime Investigations

Assumptions:
- *Among Most Complex OSI Conducts*
- *Time Sensitive*
- *High Visibility Cases*
- *High Priority Cases*
- *Impact can be*
  - *Instantaneous*
  - *Disastrous*
- *Legal Issues NOT Well Framed*

OSI Computer Crime Investigations

*Virtually **ALL** Hacker Investigations*

Start as

UNKNOWN SUBJECT *Cases*

OSI Computer Crime Investigations

Potential Subjects:

- **ALL Internet Users**

- **Anyone with**

  - **Computer, Modem, & phone**

OSI Computer Crime Investigations

What is the Internet?

Global Computer Network

- *92 Countries; Russia, Romania*
    Bulgaria, Croatia, Czech, ...
- *7,500,000 US Users*
- *15,000,000 Global Users*
- *Growth 160% per year Worldwide*
    183% per year Non-US

OSI Computer Crime Investigations

Recent Example of a Typical Intrusion Investigation:

Mar - May 94
Rome Air Development Center
Griffis AFB, NY
94IOCD96-S0008

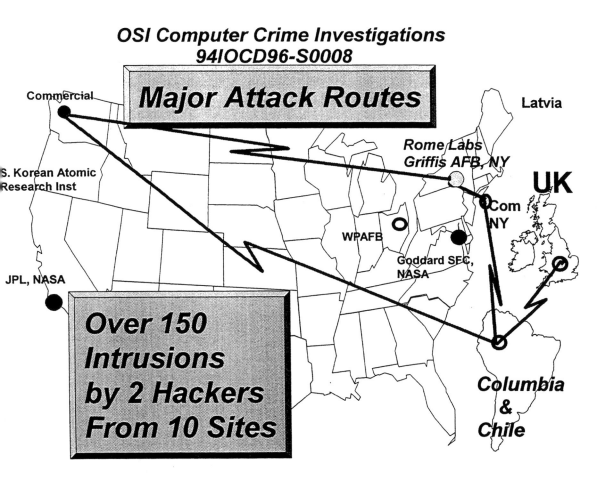

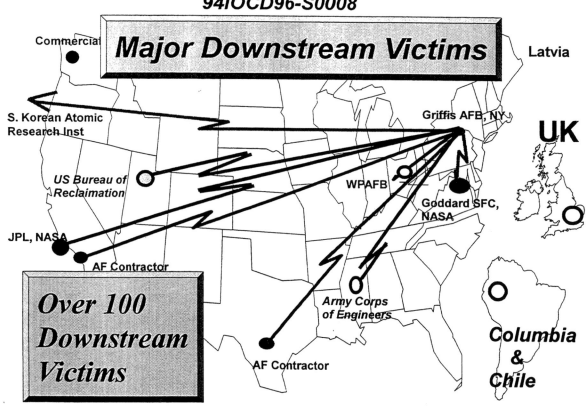

OSI Computer Crime Investigations
94IOCD96-S0008

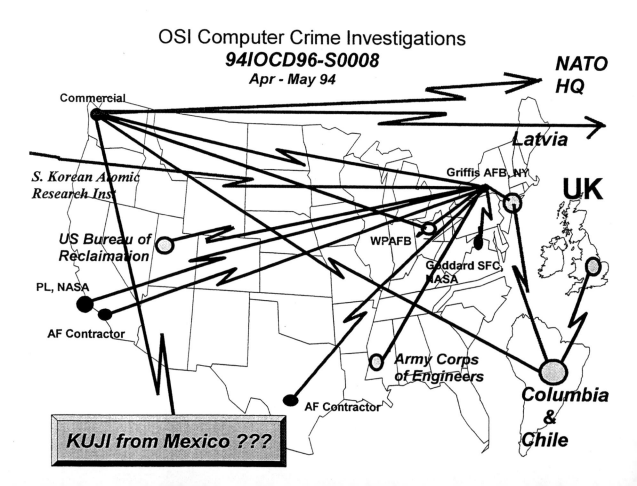

OSI Computer Crime Investigations
94IOCD96-S0008
Apr - May 94

OSI Computer Crime Investigations

Summary

- **2 Hackers**
- **26 Days of Attacks**
- **20 Days of Monitoring**
- **6 Sniffers on Rome Systems**
- **Over 150 Intrusions at ROME ADC From 10 Different Points of Origin**
- **At Least 8 Countries Used as Conduit**

OSI Computer Crime Investigations

Victims: **Air Force**
Army
Navy
NASA
Commercial Sites
DOD Contractors
Academic Sites
Other Countries

OSI Computer Crime Investigations

Investigative Jurisdictions Involved:

US Law Enforcement

FBI - Multiple Field Offices
USSS - Multiple field Offices
NASA IG
NCIS
Army CID
Army MI

Foreign Law Enforcement

New Scotland Yard, UK
Brazil
Chile

OSI Computer Crime Investigations

How It Works in OSI Now:

Sources of Allegations

1 Stop Shopping

Leads

OSI Computer Crime Investigations

How These Cases are Solved

- *Investigators With Computer Background*
- *Liaison With Other LEAs*
- *Liaison w/Computer Security*
- *Technical Surveillances*
- *Source Network*
- *Attend Hacker Conferences*

Fissile Material Proliferation

by David Kay, Vice President, Science Applications International Corporatio

ORIGINS OF THE PROBLEM

- **Break-up of the Former Soviet Union (FSU) has created new challenges for controlling the spread of fissile material and nuclear weapons**
  - → Material now on territory of four states rather than one
  - → Controls during Soviet period were primarily based on physical protection (KGB), not on technical measurements and monitoring
  - → Older nuclear weapons and most tactial nuclear weapons may have primitive safety devices – if any {ADMs, artillery rounds, etc.}
  - → Significant amounts of material not incorporated into weapons and in scattered locations (100+)
  - → Far from certain whether this material will remain under firm and responsible central control
  - → Unprecedented political, civil and economic dislocations may tempt desperate technicians, scientists, or security personnel to sell fissile materials or weapons

FISSILE MATERIAL PROLIFERATION

ORIGINS OF THE PROBLEM

- **Dismantlement of nuclear warheads will contribute to the burgeoning stockpile of weapons-usable fissile material**
  - → Concern that Russia does not have the resources for safe, secure storage of these materials.
    - ➢ Motivation behind the Cooperative Threat Reduction Program
- **Rate of dismantlement (claimed to be 1500 to 2000 warheads per year) means that it could take 15-20 years just to dismantle existing weapons**
  - → HEU could be blended down to non-weapons level and used in civil reeactors
  - → For Pu there is no final solution on how to dispose of recovered material

Very Long-Term Security Problem

FISSILE MATERIAL PROLIFERATION

ORIGINS OF THE PROBLEM

- Growing plutonium surplus world-wide resulting from operation of civilian nuclear power reactors with reprocessing
  - ➔ By the year 2000, 1000+ tons of plutonium will have accumulated worldwide in civilian spent fuel
  - ➔ By year 2000 under current plans, over 100 tons will have been separated and stored.

FISSILE MATERIAL PROLIFERATION

TRENDS

- Wake-up Call: Several incidents of "loose" nuclear material smuggled out of the FSU have already occurred
  - ➔ At least five credible cases reported in Germany since May 1994
    - ➢ Including 300 grams of 87% Pu-239 and 6 grams of 99.75% Pu-235
    - ➢ Not nearly enough to build a nuclear device, but sufficient to contaminate a large land area or water supply
  - ➔ "Nuclear Mafia" -- Apparent involvement of organized crime and former intelligence and security agents of the former Warsaw Pact
- Individually the significance of these cases is limited, but collectively they illustrate the quality and range of potential sources of supply
  - ➔ View as samples designed to generate future sales of larger amounts of fissile materials
  - ➔ View as signal of failure to control material adequately

FISSILE MATERIAL PROLIFERATION

TRENDS

- ■ **How many successful smuggling cases have gone undetected?**
  - ➔ Known seizures may be a fraction of actual transfers
- ■ **Need to be more concerned about smuggling routes to the south through the Central Asian Republics & Black Sea**
  - ➔ Weaker border control than routes to the West
  - ➔ Closer to potential clients in the Middle East
  - ➔ Bastions of criminal activity even in the Soviet period

FISSILE MATERIAL PROLIFERATION

TRENDS

"Not a single gram of plutonium 239 has gone missing from storage in Russia" -- Russian Federal Counter-Intelligence Service Press Chief Sergei Vasilyev, August 1994

"The ministry can now officially confirm that there have been no cases of the theft or disappearance of plutonium 239 from our country" -- Russian Atomic Energy Ministry Spokesman Georgy Kaurov, August 1994

"The current hullabaloo has a purely economic purpose... The West is trying to foist on us its assistance in the construction of new storage places and installation of their control systems. This would mean orders to their firms running into many millions." -- Atomic Energy Deputy Minister Yevgeny Mikerin, August 1994

The persistent tendency of some Russian officials to deny the existence of the fissile material problem is disconcerting.

FISSILE MATERIAL PROLIFERATION

- Fissile material/nuclear weapons may find its way to a nuclear black market and into the hands of aspiring proliferators
  - → Algeria, Iran, Iraq, and others
- Fissile material/nuclear weapons could be used by terrorist organizations and other sub-national groups
  - → Extortion for money or political aims
  - → Against U.S. interests abroad, friends & allies, and even CONUS

FISSILE MATERIAL PROLIFERATION

- Fissile material does not need to be utilized in an explosive device to be a threat.
  - → Disseminating even a small quantity of plutonium or other radioactive material could contaminate a large land area or water supply.
    - ➢ Imagine the ramifications if radioactive materials had been involved in the World Trade Center bombing in New York or Bishop's Gate in London

FISSILE MATERIAL PROLIFERATION

RESPONSE -- Avoid Denial

"We are not aware of what I would describe as a black market for diverted fissile material...In many cases, the people who are in possession of this diverted material have to go out an find buyers, and thankfully, we're not aware that there are that many buyers around and about" -- U.S. State Department, August 1994.

■   We can't stick our heads in the sand and pretend the problem doesn't exist. There is good reason to believe that a substantial demand for fissile materials exists. Even a rather small amount transferred into the wrong hands could pose a major threat to U.S. security interests.

FISSILE MATERIAL PROLIFERATION

RESPONSE -- Short Term

- ■ Ensure that existing stockpiles are subject to the highest standards or safety, security, and international accountability--MUCH BETTER INVENTORY
  - → Press Russians to consolidate scattered inventory of fissile material
  - → Demand that Russians apply "best available" Material Control & Accountancy Technology to fissile material inventory
  - → Cooperative Threat Reduction Program; Lab-to-Lab
- ■ Work with authorities in Russia and other countries to tighten border controls; disrupt trafficking networks and tighten security procedures at fissile material sites
  - → Russian President Boris Yeltsin has pledged Moscow's willingness to work with Germany to fight the smuggling problem
    - ➢ Tightened border control and increased intelligence exchange
  - → FBI cooperation with Russian law-enforcement agencies for a joint battle against organized crime

FISSILE MATERIAL PROLIFERATION

RESPONSE -- Mid Term

- **Minimize global accumulation of stockpiles of HEU and Pu**
  - ➔ Conclude a multilateral convention prohibiting the production of HEU or plutonium for nuclear explosive purposes.
    - ➢ U.S. has unilaterally committed to cease production
    - ➢ Russia, Great Britain, possibly France, and the Threshold States are still producing
    - ➢ Deliberations on a fissile-material cut-off are now underway at the Conference on Disarmament
      - One aim is to bring the threshold states (India, Israel, and Pakistan) under some measure of restraint
  - ➔ Encourage more restrictive regional arrangements to constrain fissile material production in regions of instability
    - ➢ Particularly Pu reprocessing

FISSILE MATERIAL PROLIFERATION

STATUS OF SNM PRODUCTION IN NWS

	Cessation of HEU Production	Cessation of PU Production
US	1964	1988: Pledge in 1991 of no plans for further production
Russia	1989	1989, 1992, & 1993 pledges to cease by 2000; 1994 bilateral PU cutoff
China	1987	1991
UK	1963	1992 statement: "production will continue to be kept at the minimum level necessary..."
France	1991-1992 (?)	1992

FISSILE MATERIAL PROLIFERATION

RESPONSE -- Mid Term

- **Pursue purchases of HEU from the FSU and other countries and its conversion to peaceful use as MOX reactor fuel.**
  - → Purchase of 500 tons of HEU from Russia already arranged
- **High priority to finding and actually implementing disposal method for Pu**
- **Explore means to limit stockpiling of plutonium from civil nuclear programs and reduce civil use of plutonium**
  - → Many of Russia's civil power reactors are major producers of plutonium and should be replaced
  - → Discourage use of civilian breeder reactors and plutonium recycling (e.g. Japan)

FISSILE MATERIAL PROLIFERATION

RESPONSE -- Long Term

- **Seek agreement among NWS to submit weapons-grade fissile material no longer in active weapons inventory to bilateral or IAEA inspection**
  - → U.S. has already set a positive precedent
    - ➢ Voluntarily put 10 tons of surplus HEU from dismantled weapons under international safeguards.
    - ➢ Plans to place some plutonium under safeguards later this year
- **Help strengthen IAEA safeguards**
  - → Support right of special inspections at undeclared facilities
  - → Lower "significant quantity" thresholds
  - → Expand intelligence resources
  - → Improve verification technologies

About the Speakers

David M. Abshire, president, CEO, and founder of the Center for Strategic and International Studies (CSIS), served as assistant secretary of state for congressional relations (1970-1973), as U.S. ambassador to NATO (1983-1987), and as special counsellor to President Reagan (1987). Dr. Abshire was a member of the Murphy Commission on the Organization of the Government for the Conduct of Foreign Policy, the President's Foreign Intelligence Advisory Board, and the President's Task Force on U.S. Government International Broadcasting. He is the recipient of many honors and awards, including the Presidential Citizens Medal and the Defense Department Medal for Distinguished Public Service.

Jack A. Blum is an internationally known attorney and a partner in Lobel, Novins, Lamont & Flug, a Washington, D.C., law firm. As a Senate investigator, he played a central role in uncovering some of the most significant international scandals of the past 20 years, including BCCI, General Manuel Noriega's drug trafficking, Lockheed Aircraft's overseas bribes, and ITT's efforts to thwart the election of Salvador Allende in Chile. He is an expert in controlling government corruption, international financial crime, money laundering, and drug trafficking. He has assisted in negotiating numerous international business transactions and has assisted clients who have been the victims of complex fraud. He has also been a consultant to the United Nations Centre on Transnational Corporations and to a number of foreign governments.

Scott Charney earned a law degree with honors from Syracuse University in 1980. Following graduation, he served for seven years as an assistant district attorney in Bronx County, New York City, the last two as a deputy chief in the Investigations Bureau. In 1987, he joined the Organized Crime and Racketeering Section of the Justice Department and was assigned to the Strike Force Field Office in Honolulu, Hawaii. In February of 1991, he transferred to the General Litigation and Legal Advice Section in Washington, D.C., and shortly thereafter he was tasked with implementing the Justice Department's Computer Crime Initiative, for which the Justice Department created a dedicated computer crime unit staffed with five federal prosecutors with Mr. Charney as chief.

In 1989, Special Agent **James Christy** was named the director of Computer Crime Investigations at the Air Force Office of Special Investigations (AFOSI), Bolling Air Force Base, Washington, D.C. As director of Computer Crime Investigations, Mr. Christy has the responsibility for management of a cadre of 21 special agents. Along with his staff, he investigates computer-related crimes and analyzes computer forensic evidence for the U.S. Air Force worldwide. AFOSI Computer Crime Investigators provide assistance and training to most Department of Defense investigative and security agencies as well as civilian law enforcement. Mr. Christy won notoriety as the original case agent in the "Hanover Hacker" case. This case involved a group of German hackers who electronically penetrated DOD computer systems all over the world and sold the information to the Soviet KGB.

Arnaud de Borchgrave is currently a senior adviser at the Center for Strategic and International Studies. During a 30-year career at *Newsweek* magazine, Mr. de Borchgrave covered most of the world's major news events. He joined the magazine in 1950 and at the age of 27 became a senior editor, a position he held for 25 years. At 21, he was appointed Brussels bureau chief for United Press International and three years later he was made *Newsweek's* bureau chief in Paris. After serving as *Newsweek's* chief European correspondent, he resigned from the magazine in 1980. His awards include Best Magazine Reporting from Abroad, Best Magazine Interpretation of Foreign Affairs, and three New York Newspaper Guild Page One Awards for foreign reporting. In 1981, Mr. de Borchgrave received the World Business Council's Medal of Honor, and in 1985 he was awarded the George Washington Medal of Honor for Excellence in Published Works. He was appointed editor in chief of the *Washington Times* and *Insight* magazine in 1985. He left his post with the *Washington Times* in 1991 and currently serves as editor at large.

Louis J. Freeh was sworn in as director of the Federal Bureau of Investigation on September 1, 1993. Prior to his appointment as director, Mr. Freeh served as an FBI Agent and an assistant U.S. attorney in the Southern District of New York. Subsequently, he held positions as chief of the Organized Crime Unit, deputy U.S. attorney, and associate U.S. attorney. During this time, Director Freeh was the lead prosecutor in the "Pizza Connection" case, the largest and most complex investigation ever undertaken by the federal government. Immediately prior to becoming head of the FBI, Director Freeh served as a U.S. District Court judge for the Southern District of New York.

L. Dain Gary has specialized in the area of computer and information security for 15 years. Currently he is the manager of the CERT Coordination Center, located at Carnegie Mellon University's Software Engineering Institute. Mr. Gary joined the CERT team from the Mellon Bank Corporation where he served as the director of Corporate Data Security. While at Mellon, he was named to the Information Systems Security Committee of the American Bankers Association and the ANSI X9F Committee, developing financial information security standards. Prior to his work in the banking industry, Mr. Gary spent four years at the National Computer Security Center as chief of the Commercial Product Evaluations Program.

Peter Grinenko is a supervisor of detectives for the Brooklyn, New York, District Attorney's Office. He is a widely acknowledged expert on the "Russian Mafia" and has been actively involved in the investigation and prosecution of Soviet and Russian criminals for the past 15 years, six of which were spent with the Federal Organized Crime Joint Task Force. He has assisted numerous law enforcement agencies, including the FBI, the DEA, the INS, U.S. Customs, the Manhattan and Queens District Attorneys' Offices, and the Latvian Police Department in their investigations of criminals from the former Soviet Union. He has also been involved in training personnel from many of these agencies in Russian criminal activities.

Carol Boyd Hallett is a leading authority on international law enforcement and trade issues. She currently serves as a trade adviser with the Clark Company of Paso Robles, California, and as a senior government relations adviser to Collier, Shannon, Rill & Scott in Washington, D.C. Previously, Mrs. Hallett was the first woman to head the United States Customs Service in its 203-year history. Appointed by President Bush, she served as commissioner from November 1989 to January 1993. During the Reagan administration, she served as U.S. ambassador to the Bahamas. Prior to these posts, Mrs. Hallett held positions as director of the U.S. Interior Department's Western Region, the director of parks and recreation for the State of California, and was elected to the California State Assembly for three terms, where she was the assembly Republican leader.

David A. Kay is assistant vice president of Science Applications International Corporation in the Negotiations and Planning Division. He has directed projects in the areas of counterproliferation, inspection and safeguarding of nuclear materials, peacekeeping, and the defense and arms control implications of developments in East Asia and the Middle East. Previously he led UN nuclear weapons inspections in post-Gulf War Iraq and for more than 15 years has been extensively involved in international activities in commercial and defense fields. He has testified frequently before Congress, and his articles have appeared in the *New York Times,* the *Washington Post,* the *Christian Science Monitor,* the *New Republic,* and a number of scholarly journals. He also has appeared on *Nightline, MacNeil-Lehrer, Today, Good Morning America,* CNN, and the evening news programs of ABC, CBS, and NBC. He has also been a frequent BBC commentator on nuclear and defense matters.

An authority on national security, counterterrorism, and crisis management, **Robert H. Kupperman** is frequently called upon as a consultant by U.S. government agencies, foreign governments, and multinational corporations. Before coming to CSIS, he was chief scientist at the U.S. Arms Control and Disarmament Agency, where he led the first interagency studies of foreign and domestic terrorism. Dr. Kupperman has also served in the Executive Office of the President, the Office of Emergency Preparedness, and as director of the transition team for the Federal Emergency Management Agency. He is the coauthor of *Terrorism: Threat, Reality, Response* (Hoover Institution Press, 1979), *Strategic Requirements for the Army to the Year 2000* (Lexington Books, 1984), and *Final Warning* (Doubleday, 1989). He has a Ph.D. in applied mathematics from New York University and has taught at the University of Maryland and New York University.

He is currently a senior adviser at the Center for Strategic and International Studies.

Senator Patrick Leahy of Burlington was elected to the U.S. Senate in 1974 and remains the only Democrat ever elected to this office from Vermont. Prior to his election, Senator Leahy served for eight years as state's attorney in Vermont's largest county (Chittenden). He gained a national reputation for his law enforcement activities and was selected in 1974 as one of three outstanding prosecutors in the United States. The senator chairs the Appropriations Subcommittee on Foreign Operations and the Judiciary Subcommittee on Technology and the Law. He is also former vice chairman of the Senate Select Committee on Intelligence. As chairman of the Subcommittee on Technology and the Law, Leahy paved the way for the United States to become part of the Berne Convention, the world's leading international copyright agreement. He has initiated hearings on computer viruses, electronic spying, technological piracy, and high tech terrorism.

Dr. Rensselaer Lee is president of Global Advisory Services, an Alexandria, Va. firm that consults on international development, narcotics control, and national security issues. He is concurrently an associate scholar at the Foreign Policy Research Institute in Philadelphia, Pa. He has consulted widely for the U.S. government and for multinational corporations. Dr. Lee has written extensively on problems of narcotics, crime, and political change in Eurasia and Latin America and is the author of *The White Labyrinth: Cocaine and Political Power* (Transaction Publishers, 1989). He is currently working on a book on organized crime and political development in the former Soviet Union.

William R. McLucas was named director of the Division of Enforcement at the Securities and Exchange Commission by Chairman Richard C. Breeden in December of 1989. The Enforcement Division of the Commission is responsible for civil and administrative prosecution of those who violate the federal securities law. Before being named director, Mr. McLucas was an associate director of the division. Since he joined the commission in 1977, he has held a number of different positions, including staff attorney, branch chief, and assistant director, and was named associate director in 1985. Prior to joining the commission, he was an attorney with the Federal Home Loan Bank Board and is admitted to the bar of the Supreme Court of Pennsylvania.

Ronald D. Murphy is the director of the Advanced Systems Technology Office (ASTO) of the Advanced Research Projects Agency (ARPA), where he is responsible for a variety of advanced systems development and demonstration programs in the areas of aeronautics, space, precision strike, land systems, counter drug, intelligence, and advanced distributed simulation. Prior to joining ARPA, Mr. Murphy worked as an engineer at Boeing, at the U.S. Air Force Flight Dynamics Laboratory, and in the U.S. Navy. He has directed numerous advanced technology aircraft design studies and projects including the XFV-12A, the A-6E STOL demonstrator, the AV-8B Radar Demonstrator, and ARPA's advanced Unmanned Air Vehicle activities.

Donn B. Parker, a senior management systems consultant, has spent 24 of his 42 years in the computer field at SRI International working in information security. He is the founder at SRI of the International Information Integrity Institute (I-4), continuously serving more than 60 of the largest multinational corporations in the world for more than eight years in the protection of their information assets. Mr. Parker has led the National Science Foundation grant-funded studies on ethical conflicts in computer science, technology, and business in 1977 and 1987. He is a world-renowned consultant, lecturer, writer, and researcher on computer crime and security issues. He has written five books on computer crime, ethics, and information security management. Mr. Parker has been the consulting editor of the *Journal of Information Security* since 1992. He is also the author of the *Criminal Justice Resource Manual on Computer Crime,* available from the U.S. National Institute of Justice, and coauthor of *Ethical Conflicts in Computer Science, Technology, and Business,* published in 1990 by QED Information Sciences, Inc.

As vice president and director of studies at the Center for Strategic and International Studies, **Erik Peterson** oversees the development and execution of the Center's broad-based research agenda. He came to the Center from Kissinger Associates, where he was director of research and head of the firm's Washington, D.C., office. Mr. Peterson was inaugural coeditor of the *SAIS Review* and is the author of *The Gulf Cooperation Council: Search for Unity in a Dynamic Region* and of the chapter entitled "The Outlook for the GCC in the Postwar Gulf" in J.E. Peterson, ed., *Saudi*

Arabia and the Gulf States. He holds a B.A. in international affairs from Colby College, a Certificate of Eastern European Studies from the University of Fribourg in Switzerland, an M.A. in international law and economics from the Paul H. Nitze School of Advanced International Studies at the Johns Hopkins University, and an M.B.A. in finance and international business from the Wharton School of the University of Pennsylvania.

Robert H. Rasor is a 24-year veteran with the U.S. Secret Service, having served in St. Louis, New York City, and Washington, D.C., in protective, investigative, and staff assignments. Currently, Mr. Rasor is in charge of the Financial Crimes Division of the U.S. Secret Service Headquarters in Washington, D.C. This division is responsible for the worldwide oversight, direction, and coordination of criminal investigations dealing with financial institution fraud, access device/credit card/telemarketing fraud, computer/ telecommunications fraud, E.F.T. Fraud, Nigerian/Asian organized crime, false identification, and other related crimes.

Having recently retired from the Federal Bureau of Investigation, **Oliver "Buck" Revell** is the founder and president of The Revell Group International, Inc., a global business and security consulting firm. Throughout his 30-year career with the FBI, Mr. Revell directed numerous initiatives and divisions on organized crime and served as the director's principal deputy for criminal investigations, counterterrorism and counterintelligence. He was also responsible for all international investigative liaison activities, and was a member of the National Foreign Intelligence Board, the Terrorist Crisis Management Center, the Deputy's Committee of the National Security Council. He commanded the joint FBI/CIA operation, Operation Goldenrod, which led to the first apprehension of an international terrorist overseas.

An internationally acclaimed journalist and author, **Claire Sterling** has covered numerous stories including the Algerian war of liberation, the Suez War, the Six-Day War, the Nigerian civil war, and, while a foreign correspondent in Italy, she regularly reported on political developments in Italy and western Europe. Since 1980, she has devoted all her time to writing books on organized crime, terrorism, intelligence, and political corruption. Her books include *The Masaryk Case* (Harper & Row), *The Terror Network* (Holt, Reinhart), *The Time of the Assassins* (Holt, Reinhart), *Octopus: The Long Reach of the Sicilian Mafia* (W.W. Norton), and, most recently, *Thieve's World: The New Global Threat of Organized Crime* (Simon & Schuster), which exposes the influence of Russian organized crime and its new international connections.

Since joining the Metropolitan Police 30 years ago, **David C. Veness** has commanded a number of different departments, ranging from hostage negotiating to criminal intelligence. Mr. Veness is presently the assistant commissioner of the Metropolitan Police, New Scotland Yard, where he is responsible for serious, organized, and international crime, the fraud squad, the flying squad, the crime operations branch, criminal intelligence and firearms. He is also secretary of the Chief Officers Committee of the South East Regional Crime Squad.

William H. Webster was sworn in as Director of Central Intelligence (DCI) on May 26, 1987. As director, he headed the Intelligence Community (all foreign intelligence agencies of the United States) and directed the Central Intelligence Agency until September 1, 1991. After a career as a practicing attorney and as a U.S. attorney, he was appointed a judge of the U.S. District Court for the Eastern District of Missouri and was elevated to the U.S. Court of Appeals for the Eighth Circuit. He resigned in 1978 to become director of the FBI. In 1991, Webster was the recipient of the Distinguished Medal, the Presidential Medal of Freedom, and the National Security Medal. In September 1991, he joined the law firm of Milbank, Tweed, Hadley & McCloy in its Washington, D.C. office.

R. James Woolsey was sworn in as Director of Central Intelligence (DCI) on February 5, 1993. In this position he heads the Intelligence Community (all foreign intelligence agencies of the United States) and directs the Central Intelligence Agency. Prior to his appointment as DCI, Mr. Woolsey served as the general counsel to the U.S. Senate Committee on Armed Services, the under secretary of the Navy, the ambassador and U.S. representative to the Negotiation on Conventional Armed Forces in Europe (CFE), and as a partner of the law firm Shea & Gardner. He has served on a number of presidential commissions and has been a trustee of the Center for Strategic and International Studies.